symbolism

the glory of escutcheoned doors

MARK PATRICK HEDERMAN

VERITAS

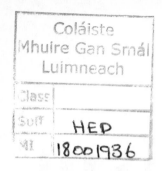
First published 2007 by
Veritas Publications
7/8 Lower Abbey Street
Dublin 1
Ireland
Email publications@veritas.ie
Website www.veritas.ie

ISBN 978 1 85390 937 5

A catalogue record for this book is available from the British Library.

All scripture quotes are from the *New Revised Standard Version Bible*: Catholic Edition © 1993
and 1998 by the Division of Christian Education of the National Council of the Churches of
Christ in the United States of America. Used with permission. All rights reserved.

'What Then?', 'Byzantium' and 'Sailing to Byzantium' by W.B. Yeats are used by permission of
AP Watt Ltd on behalf of Gráinne Yeats.

Self Portrait with Bandaged Ear, 1889 by Gogh, Vincent van (1853-90) © Samuel
Courtauld Trust, Courtauld Institute of Art Gallery/The Bridgeman Art Library; The Yellow
House, 1888 (oil on canvas) by Gogh, Vincent van (1853-90) © Van Gogh Museum,
Amsterdam, The Netherlands/The Bridgeman Art Library; Starry Night, 1889 (oil on
canvas) by Gogh, Vincent van (1853-90) © Museum of Modern Art, New York, USA/The
Bridgeman Art Library; Sunflowers, 1888 by Gogh, Vincent van (1853-90) © National
Gallery, London, UK/The Bridgeman Art Library; The Dead Christ, 1521 (tempera on
panel) by Holbein, Hans the Younger (1497/8-1543) © Kunstmuseum, Basel, Switzerland/
The Bridgeman Art Library; The Ambassadors, 1533 (oil on panel) by Holbein, Hans the
Younger (1497/8-1543) © National Gallery, London, UK/The Bridgeman Art Library

Designed by Colette Dower
Printed in the Republic of Ireland by Betaprint, Dublin

*Veritas books are printed on paper made from the wood pulp of managed forests. For every
tree felled, at least one tree is planted, thereby renewing natural resources.*

Through a chink too wide there comes in no wonder.

PATRICK KAVANAGH, 'ADVENT'

Earth's crammed with heaven,
And every common bush afire with God;
But only he who sees, takes off his shoes –
The rest sit round it and pluck blackberries.

ELIZABETH BARRETT BROWNING, *AURORA LEIGH*, BOOK VII

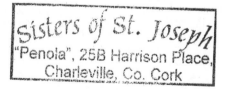

To John and Josephine,

1907–2007

Moonlight and Roses

Three years of Creative Writing plus two years of 'Liturgy and Life' at Glenstal Abbey, several seminars at Dalgan Park and Kiltegan, with a summer stay at le Chateau de Lavigny in Switzerland in July 2006, have provided whatever focus is present in these pages.

Maura Hyland, Fanny Howe and Anna Bourgeois
have forced my hand.

Knockfierna, Cloonty and Cappercullen have provided the landscape. You, dear reader, will have to supply the rest.

Thank you for your patience,

Mark Patrick

Contents

Introduction:
Portals of Discovery

I wrote this book in order to relate an important secret which I have discovered during my time in this world. I believe that I was guided to this discovery and led by the hand until I did so. The discovery itself is intimately linked with my own life story and the telling of it intertwined with the telling of that story. Any person can make such a discovery quite independently of their own life story and quite otherwise than mine. In fact, the mingling of these two realities may be as irritating to some as it could be helpful to others. I know no way of communicating this mystery to my reader other than by combining it with the story of my own discovery of it.

And so, what is the discovery? It is about experiencing this world symbolically. The energy of God takes over as the operating fuel in human personality. This happens and perdures through a life of symbols. In other words, symbols are the cause and the continuity of such a life. However, it also means that you begin to experience the world symbolically, that the world around you is a front or a sign of a greater reality. This means that symbols are also the result of such a life. From this perspective the most important symbol of all is you yourself as an active part in a greater whole.

Symbols are particles buried in one reality which bespeak their connection to, or with, a greater reality. When I say that you are a symbol I mean that apart from the biological, chronological, geographically located identity that is you, who were born on a certain date, occupied a certain space on the planet and fulfilled a very specific and recorded *curriculum vitae* during your lifetime until you died and were buried on another specific and identifiable date, there is a bigger and better and much more important 'you' which far exceeds this meagre and quantifiable slice of existence. In fact this historical you is merely an appetiser, a soupçon, an inkling, an intimation of the you who is infinite, eternal and everlastingly you. So, the most important discovery about your life story is that you yourself are a living symbol.

You are not, as most of us imagine and are taught, the whole reality of who you are – you are simply the preview. Everything about you, everything that happens to you, everything that you are, is indicative of what you could be, of what you are in another dimension. If you could see yourself in the perspective of infinity, in the time warp of eternity, you would recognise that what you experience as one horizontal thread in the three dimensional tapestry of human history is, from the obverse angle, a harmonic note in a larger, deeper matrix.

Accustomed as we are to the anchored swivel range of the human viewpoint we have to imagine the alternative space and time which makes of every element within the created world, including ourselves, a meaningful part of a very much greater whole. Far from being a star upon the curtain of the firmament, we are portholes in a submarine ploughing through an ocean of infinity. Such a viewpoint turns everything we think we see into a symbol of something else, something larger.

Let me think of a crude example. Two people meet at 6 a.m. on a Monday morning in front of a bank. It is raining slightly. They talk to one another for a few minutes. The second person then moves away and the first takes up position on a chair in a porch. This person is a guard replacing the other on a morning shift. Unbeknownst to either, their meeting is the signal which a second group has given to begin robbing this bank. Their meeting is the catalyst for a much more sophisticated and diverse series of manoeuvres involving several others who have been previously preparing for this moment and this sign.

However, in the meantime, a secret agent – planted within the gang and working for an international anti-terrorist organisation – has alerted headquarters who have also specified this morning meeting of the two people as the signal for putting into operation their swoop on the gang whom they have been following for some months. Up to now they have not had an opportunity to catch the robbers red-handed.

Thus the very mundane meeting of two people on a Monday morning at 6 a.m. suddenly takes on a much larger meaning. It becomes part of at least two other sets of significance which weave into a multilayered tapestry. With hindsight, these two people can look back at their very ordinary fulfilment of a daily routine and become aware that on at least one morning, their lives took on a significance which made every action they performed into something momentous.

In something of a similar fashion our everyday lives are embroiled in at least two larger plans of action. There is a force of evil which tries to bring every human endeavour towards annihilation, but there is also a beneficent and evolutionary influence, acting at all times through designated human beings, who are secret agents for this creative centre of gravity. Everything we do happens at the epicentre of such a crossroads. So, even our life here on earth is not something which we take in hand and forge for ourselves as if we were inside it and guiding it like the captain of a submarine viewing the past and the future through the lens of a periscope. It begins much further back than that and its significance is registered on a much wider skin surface than the radar screen of our internal consciousness. There is a preparation for our arrival which concerns the history of two families, two members of which eventually give birth to that visible, tangible, recordable flightpath which is our biographical life. This one life represents a number of seconds in the overall chronology of the planet. But every preparation for that life, every coincidental collision of possibility which produced it, every external, temporal accident or action which formed it, governed it, directed, shaped and concluded it, are symbolic tangents representing a larger, wiser, more comprehensive pattern which we describe in our limited vocabulary as eternal, infinite, everlasting.

Such words are merely projected opposites of the short, limited and fragile existence we experience both in ourselves and all around us on the planet during the brief moment of our stay here. But they are based upon the glimpses which we get of that deeper, broader, wider horizon which flashes its light off the reflective surface of those precious gems which we are, in our deepest selves and which every element of this creation *is* at its most crucial, its most sacramental. We and they are symbols of an alternative energy, a subterranean biology more lively than any we have been able to identify on this obverse side of our shortchanging hemisphere.

Our biological life from birth to death is bankrolled by counterfeit currency unless we consciously switch to the alternative energy of divine illumination. In light of this superior wattage we ourselves and everything that exists in our world are seen, heard, tasted, smelled, touched, and breathed, not as discrete, self-contained things in themselves but as manifestations of a larger reality, signals from a vaster energy.

Part One:

Biography

Gemini

I was in Germany visiting the monastery of Maria Laach at Christmas time during the winter of 1969. One of the monks there told me that he could see two people in me. He was a professional photographer and offered to take two pictures which would show me the two people. I went to his studio and he asked me to walk around casually and ignore him while he took many shots from different angles. He didn't show me all the photographs he had taken. He picked out two which were quite strikingly, as I saw them, my father and my mother respectively. He had recognised the two inmates lodged within, of whom I was the symbolic summary. I am myself, certainly. But I am also the symbol of their love for one another.

My father, John Hederman (1907–1984), was the youngest son in a family of five. He inherited one of the family farms, three hundred and fifty acres at Ballyneale, Co. Limerick. He was supposed to marry a girl whose sister had married my uncle and who had inherited the original family farm next door. Presumably the marriage had been arranged by his parents.

My mother, Josephine Mullaney (1907–1987), was born in Boston, Massachussetts, six months after my father in the same year. Her father died young, apparently in the great 'flu epidemic, and her mother, who was Irish, preferred to take her chances in the home country rather than remain in the American city where her husband had made quite a tidy fortune.

She and her three children sailed for Dublin on the Cunard line in the 1930s. My mother went to Trinity College where she studied for an arts degree.

Soon after, she was invited to spend ten days at Ballyneale by my father's sister, who lived there. My mother was at first reluctant to go but was stung into acceptance by her siblings, who said she was a stick-in-the-mud and never went anywhere.

My father was walking down the front avenue and saw his sister coming through the gate in a car. He ignored her completely as was his wont until he saw someone else in the car with her, Josephine. It was love at first sight. A few days later my father proposed to my mother. 'I know nothing about you,' she said, somewhat dismissively. His was the thirteenth such proposal she had dismissed to date. 'You know as much about me now as you'll ever know,' came the jaunty reply, 'so, you'd better make up your mind.' Both witnesses agreed some fifty years later that he was right! They never did get to know much more about each other.

And yet they remained 'in love'. What they saw in each other was beyond what either of them ever reached or understood in their own lives. It was a dream, a hope. Both of them were physically beautiful. My father was well-built and tall, my mother intelligently glamorous and petite. People said that they looked like each other and could have been brother and sister. On my father's side this 'love' was a very deep infatuation, an admiration close to idolatry. On my mother's side it was probably a mixture of deep gratitude for his overwhelming and very physical love, allied to an irrevocable decision she had carefully and prayerfully taken, enshrined in a deeply religious belief in the marriage vows they had sworn to each other.

Such slender and fragile threads of chance organised my arrival on a Co. Limerick farm in 1944. I was the result of this meteoric collision between two fragments of the galaxy. But there was more to it than that: their marriage had also been arranged so that a future person could be fashioned out of the instinct for communion which brought them together so fortuitously. As such, I was the symbol of their potential future, their dream, destined to work out inside my own intestines the peace treaty which they kept postponing and which such distances and differences inevitably generate. They were two separate people who could afford to circumnavigate each other during their lifetime; I was a combination of both who had to come to terms with their circuitous dance.

I hardly ever spoke with my father without there being a third person in the room. Neither of us would have wanted it any other way. We played golf together and he applauded and enjoyed everything I achieved even when others disapproved. 'Ride on, Marcus!' was his perennial and encouraging cry. We got on well and enjoyed each other's company – albeit somewhat reticently. He sometimes attracted people who hoped to confide in him. He was embarrassed and nonplussed by such overtures and diplomatically demurred; he wasn't at all into baring his soul.

My mother, on the other hand, was a deep communicator with those she counted as her friends. When I was eighteen I decided to approach her directly. I told her that I wanted to be her friend, not just her son. I was sure we could really get to know one another if we made the effort. She was clear and decisive. 'My generation,' she told me, 'values courtesy, where yours seems to value intimacy. The two idioms cannot mix. I never met a man in my life without spending several hours preparing myself to do so. You young people go off camping together without even a chaperone. How can one have any respect for someone you meet crawling out of a tent in a sleeping bag before breakfast in the morning?'

I gave up. It wasn't just a battle of the sexes, it was a generation gap.

Parallel lines, mathematicians tell us, meet in infinity, as parents can meet, if and when their children break through to this dimension. What some beneficent evolutionary appetite sows as seeds of passion in the past, become composite living creatures in the present, undertaking to realise a dream in the future. John and Josephine's dream became my vocation: to turn the key in the lock of eternity and open a door into the infinite. When I talk about symbolism I mean two things represented in one thing. This one thing is all that can be seen in this world but it encompasses and gives access to the much larger reality of which it is both offspring and replica. At all times and in all places of our history and geography we are being pushed, seduced, shepherded towards this breach in the bulwarks of the supposedly escape-proof workaday world.

Annapurnas
of the Mind

It was summer and I saw him getting out of a large black car. He was tall, strongly built, sun-tanned, golden-haired, sure of himself. I was nine, he was eighteen; twice my age and size. He once saved my brother from drowning when he first came to Ireland a year or so after I was born. He was my hero. A blond god from America who had come originally with his parents to visit our farm in southern Ireland. They were friends of my mother. Americans were different. Outspoken, better fed, flamboyant, exaggerated: characters from a story book. There was a whiff of adventure about them. John Harlin was their only son.

This time he had come on his own. He treated me like an adult. We talked about things we already knew. He wanted to climb mountains; I wanted to find God. He said he didn't believe in God as such but that mountains provided the nearest thing to divinity he had ever experienced. We said we would keep in touch. Years later, in March 1966, six months after I had made solemn profession as a monk in the Benedictine Order, I heard that he was to climb the front face of the Eiger mountain in Switzerland. The name of the mountain comes from the word 'ogre' in certain vocabularies. This mountain had claimed many lives. By this time he was married with two children and had become famous enough to have *The Sunday Telegraph* cover the expedition.

He had climbed the north face of the Matterhorn aged twenty, graduated as top pilot of his class in the US Air Force, and flew in the USAF formation flying team. He had worked for Balmain as a dress designer. What contrasts! Who was this man? What drove him to the Eiger? He was searching for something, he said, something he thought he could find by climbing mountains.

As he neared the summit, the most triumphant moment of his life, the rope holding him to the mountainside broke and he fell four thousand feet to his death in the snowfields of Kleine Scheidegg. His face appeared on the front page of the coloured supplement to the *Weekend Telegraph* on 29 April 1966. He was wearing a red shirt and staring at the famous profile of the Eiger mountain which claimed his life at the age of thirty.

Dougal Haston, the only member of the Harlin team to reach the top, with Peter Gillman, the journalist covering the climb, published a book about it in the same year: *Direttissima, The Eiger Assault: The Climb That Made the World Hold its Breath*. This *direttissima* route to the summit of the Eiger is now known as the Harlin route.

John's devastated parents wanted someone to write the whole story, the real purpose of their son's life. They hired the greatest mountaineering writer of the time, James Ramsay Ullman, who had recounted the conquest of Everest by Edmund Hilary and Tenzing Norgay, to tell the story of their son. They paid him and all his expenses for two years while he researched and wrote. This author had never met John Harlin, but he visited everyone who knew him, and retraced his footsteps around the world. He interviewed us in our family home. Two years later he had completed his task. He sent the text to John's parents. They were not happy. The author's conclusion was that John Harlin's purpose in climbing mountains was to get as far away as possible from them, especially from his mother.

Rear Admiral John Harlin, Senior, and Sue, his wife, told James Ramsay Ullman that they would rather not have the book published, that they were withdrawing their request. They learned very quickly that in law the book belongs to the person who writes it and not to those who commissioned or sponsored it. The biography appeared in 1968. James Ramsay Ullman called it *Straight Up*: 'a way of serving a drink, of climbing a mountain, of living a life.' For John Harlin II, the author told his readers, 'there was no other way.' Ullman used the *Weekend Telegraph* picture as an inset on the front cover, and had a larger photograph of himself on the back cover. The copy of this book, which I now have in front of me, carries a handwritten note on the inside flyleaf from John's mother to my mother:

> We are not completely happy with this book, especially the manner in which the author has treated John's relationship with his mother and father. Those of you who knew all of us will be able to make your own assessment.

It was a lesson for me. No one should be hired from outside to define the purpose of your life. You have to reserve that privilege for yourself. John and his parents had somehow been portrayed in a way that hurt them. Later, I noticed that the book was dedicated to Marilyn, John's widow. Accurate perspectives are not always gleaned from your daughter-in-law.

* * *

> O the mind, mind has mountains; cliffs of fall
> Frightful, sheer, no-man-fathomed. Hold them cheap
> May who ne'er hung there.[1]

Forty years later as I planned to write this book, two strange things happened. I was searching the Internet when a picture of the Eiger mountain appeared on the screen. It was an advertisement for *The Alps: Giants of Nature*, an IMAX film coming to giant screen theatres in the Spring of 2007. The name John Harlin appeared on the screen and I knew the promptings were coming from another source.

John Harlin III had reached the summit of the north face of the Eiger mountain forty years after his father had died there. With him were the European climbers Robert and Daniela Jasper. The team reached the summit on 24 September 2005 after a climb that lasted three days. They bivouacked on the mountain for two nights.

John Harlin III was nine years old when his father died. 'I am relieved, after so many years, to have finally made my peace with the Eiger,' said Harlin III, now aged forty-nine. 'The Eiger has cast a shadow over my family for decades, and while this climb does not change the fact of my father's death, it allows me personally to close a significant chapter in my life.'

I was invited to Switzerland to give a talk and a workshop in Flüeli-Ranft on Thursday, 13 July 2006. As I gave my workshop on synchronicity using the story of John Harlin and his son as one of my examples, more than twenty million cubic feet of stone from the east face of the Eiger mountain fell hundreds of feet in a thundering fifteen-minute avalanche. Earlier that day the hundred-foot-high rock formation of the Eiger, known as the Madonna, collapsed. No one was injured and no buildings were hit in the rock fall. The glacial ice, which had been holding the mountain in place for centuries, had melted. The front face of the Eiger which towers over Grindewald with a mile-high sheer wall and a summit at 13,025 feet had melted and it may now be impossible for anyone else ever again to undertake the Harlin route.

None of this has allowed me to make peace with my own Eiger Mountain but it has taught me several lessons in mountaineering. Life is mostly a mountain climb. The mountain for me was an internal one in the same way that

Gerard Manley Hopkins describes above. The fact that, as I used this story to describe such symbolism, a son of John Harlin's should appear on my screen doing what his father had done forty years before, and that the ogre which both of them had to overcome, each in their own way and in their own time, should melt before our eyes, illustrates three aspects of symbolism which should, I hope, become apparent throughout the pages of this book. There is a contemporaneity about symbolism which makes it always present to you as you are now. There is another energy, a higher presence, working with you in every step you take. And there is a reality of, in, and for, today with regard to symbolism which is made present in a time and space other than the temporal and the geographical. Both the Madonna and the mountain will survive.

Knockfierna

Before he went to school
he could read the bark of trees,
leaf veins,
seashell-convolutions,
footprints,
and the touch of fingers;
now he goes to school,
and he can only read words.
JENNIFER FARLEY

My awareness of symbols came from my childhood. I did not go
to school until I was nine years of age as my American mother
believed that children should not go to school until they
themselves asked to do so. So the first nine years of my life were
spent roaming the hillsides of west Limerick with my sister,
Louise, mostly on ponies. We lived on a farm and close by was
Knockfierna, a large hill in the middle distance between us and
the Galtee mountains. The whole countryside of Ireland is a
network of healing and sacred places embedded in the psychic
memory of the land. In sight of the Galtee mountains, between
the rivers Deel and Maigue a ridge of old red sandstone rises
abruptly from the limestone land of the surrounding area. This
is *Cnoc Fírinne* (Hill of Truth) and is almost one thousand feet
high. It was a short distance from our farm. Most of my
childhood was spent in its vicinity. It had a cairn on top: a large

heap of stones added to by those who climb the hill. This cairn was called *An Buachaill Bréagach* (the deceitful boy). Near this cairn is an opening known as *Poll na Bruíne* which was an entrance to the underworld, the palace beneath the hill (*Brú na Bruíne*) where Donn Fíreannach presided. This word *Brú* occurs also in the names of towns in the locality, Bruree and Bruff for instance, and refers to such underground hostels as are found at the great megalithic site in the Boyne valley known as *Brú na Bóinne*. Many people around Ballingarry believed that there were underground tunnels from *Cnoc Fírinne* to the mouth of the Shannon, and up towards Tory Hill and beyond.

West Limerick is a place of high ringfort density south of the Shannon estuary. There was a ring fort on a forty acre field at the edge of our own farm and a second one at Ballingarry Down on the approach to Knockfierna. I spent much time in both these places. Although it has been suggested that such forts were occupied from the Bronze Age (1,800 BCE) more recent and more accurate dendrochronology and radiocarbon dating point to a period between 600 and 900 CE for the construction of most ringforts around Ireland.[1] Whatever about their chronology or their construction, these were openings to another world. I later discovered that all cultures, and most children throughout the world, believe in the existence of such a second dimension. In Africa the anthills of the Savannah were another variety of such openings. Knockfierna itself was the palace of Donn Fíreannach, god of the dead and of the fertility of the land, who was generally seen in our area on horseback.

A cross-country hurling match between the *Slua Sí* of *Cnoc Fírinne* led by Donn and the *Slua Sí* of Lough Gur and *Cnoc Áine* (Knockainey) led by the goddess Áine took place every Autumn. The ball would be thrown in half-way between the two places, about fifteen miles between Knockfierna and Knockainey. If Donn succeeded in driving the ball back to Knockfierna the crops in this part of the country would thrive, but if Áine got the upper hand the people of Ballingarry could look out for themselves.

There is an account of Cearúil Ó Dálaigh, composer of *Eilín a Rún*, travelling to Kilmallock to get Eilín to elope with him: he noticed a white horse going up the hill of *Cnoc Fírinne*. He followed it to the *Poll Dubh* where he found a horse grazing but no sign of its rider. He threw a stone down the *Poll na Bruíne*. It was thrown back hitting him in the face and breaking his nose.

An old man who worked for my father told me that coming back from church in Granagh he heard 'fairy' music. As he looked through the low open window of his room out on Knockfierna, he knew that he would be there soon on the whale-backed Black Hill beside.

When I did eventually go to school it was quite a shock to be surrounded by other children. Being at school teaches us to be like children and to act that age. If you have lived all your life with adults you are not aware of the idiom. But you learn very quickly. I reverted to childhood within weeks. But the teachers here had no interest whatsoever in Donn Fíreannach or his *buachaill bréagach*. In fact they regarded all that as nonsense at the best of times and as heresy at the worst of times. And they had their ways of dealing with heretics. Every teacher in the school was armed with a different kind of sceptre or crozier for beating out heresy and converting the pagans. Pagans and heathens, I later learned, were all those who lived in the countryside (*paganus*) and dwelt on the heaths. As so many before me I went into hiding like Heathcliff and became, as Jacob and Ulysses, a deceitful boy. At school there was only one world. It was measured by geometry (which means, in Greek, 'measuring the world') and counted in numbers which contained no magic. We sat in serried rows like passive clones for nine hours every day, supervised for the most part by one other person who brainwashed us continuously and beat us if we objected. Nine hours were spent asleep in dormitories and the remaining time was divided into organised games, meals or prayer. The object was to help us 'get ahead' in the workaday world. We learned to read and write and then began the scientific conquest of the space-time continuum in which we lived. Of course there was only one kind of space and only one kind of time. Both were absolute and invariant. There was no question of space being beyond us or time being inside us, no understanding of my space or your space, no appreciation of music as time being 'felt' or made audible, no such thing as time-for-us.

This was an inventory of intelligible locations and dates, a map of the world for anthropologists anonymous. If you were living in any other kind of space and time, you were a dreamer, an idler, a good-for-nothing. The space we all lived in was an ordered totality of concrete extensions, the time we lived in was an ordered totality of concrete durations. Space, time and motion had been calculated for us; all we had to do was learn off the formulae. There was no time or space for 'my' world or 'your' world, for an overworld or an underworld – we were dealing with the 'real' world. We measured this in metres, kilograms and seconds. The distance from Knockfierna to the ringfort was to be calculated in units which were one ten-millionth part of the meridian which passes from the pole to the equator. It didn't matter what anyone felt like, or what was going on underneath the ground. All that was subjective and personal. What we were after was an objective assessment: a picture of the world from nobody's point of view. If you arrive in London you don't want a sentimentally biased account of what someone else thinks you should see, you want a map which will show you where one should go and how to get there.

By the time I left school, of course, this attempt to reduce the world to signs and symbols which were unambiguous, incontravertible and universally accepted had already been changed. Just after my sixteenth birthday the standardised MKS of my rigid schooldays had been revised. The mouth of the *Poll*

Dubh on *Cnoc Fírinne* was now to be measured in metres which were more accurately and scientifically accepted to be 1,650,753.73 wavelengths of the orange-red light of krypton 86.

The school I went to held a retreat every year for boarders. We were asked to remain silent for three days and if we did so we would be given a free day at the end by the headmaster. Behind the main building there was a cultivated garden with a view of the Sugarloaf in Wicklow. This was supposed to be one of the most beautiful views in the country. It was too much of a picture postcard for me. It had nothing of the magic of Knockfierna. We could use the garden during the retreat to say the rosary as we walked up and down. The way in which we said the rosary was unusual. We divided ourselves into two teams. One team would begin saying the rosary and the other would attack them and bring them to the ground, shoving their faces into the earth until the rosary was silenced. When eventually all sound of the rosary had been eliminated, it was the turn of the second team to stand up and begin the recital until they, in turn, had been reduced to silence. In this way we fulfilled our obligations to pray without forfeiting our free day at the end by breaking the silence.

The retreat master, Fr Gabriel Harty, was known as 'the rosary priest'. After he had given his first talk about saying 'the howly rowsary to save your sowl', I went to him and told him that he wasn't getting through to these boys at all. If he would let me give the next talk I would be able to tell them all about God in a way they might understand. He was very kind and told me that his next talk was going to involve showing a series of slides and that I could help him man the slide projector. School taught me huge parsimony of pity – there were so many people to be pitied in the world.

Knowledge of God was communicated through a *Catechism of Catholic Doctrine*, approved by the Archbishops and Bishops of Ireland, with an imprimatur from John Charles McQuaid, dated 2 February 1951. This catechism was learnt off by heart.

The book was printed and bound in the Republic of Ireland. It began with 'The Sign of the Cross' and continued with four hundred and forty-three questions starting with 'Who made the world?' And 'Who is God?' And ending with 'What are exorcisms?' A local priest with a bamboo cane beat the answers into those who were slow or uninterested. I knew all the questions with their answers by rote and still do. They had very little, if anything, to do with my conversations on Knockfierna.

* * *

What Then?

> His chosen comrades thought at school
> He must grow a famous man;
> He thought the same and lived by rule,
> All his twenties crammed with toil;
> 'What then?' sang Plato's ghost. 'What then?'
>
> Everything he wrote was read,
> After certain years he won
> Sufficient money for his need,
> Friends that have been friends indeed;
> 'What then? sang Plato's ghost. 'What then?'
>
> All his happier dreams came true –
> A small old house, wife, daughter, son,
> Grounds where plum and cabbage grew,
> Poets and wits about him drew;
> 'What then?' sang Plato's ghost. 'What then?'
>
> 'The work is done,' grown old he thought,
> 'According to my boyish plan;
> Let the fools rage, I swerved in naught,
> Something to perfection brought';
> But louder sang that ghost, 'What then?'[2]

W.B. YEATS

Kathleen Raine, who was born in 1908 and who died at the age of ninety-five in the year 2003, summed herself up and the century through which she had lived as follows:[3]

> [As a] child of my time, who at Cambridge read Natural Sciences, and rejected my Christian heritage in order to adopt with uncritical zeal the current scientific orthodoxy of that university, I have lived long enough to come full circle. It is all that I learned in my Cambridge days that I have little by little come to reject, by a reversal of premisses which has brought me to my own Orient. A slow learner, I have been blessed with a long life which has brought me to a knowledge not taught in our schools.

Have we taken a wrong turn somewhere along the line? If so, when did this happen, and what can we do about it now?

Many believe that we have taken a wrong turn. They look around them at the kind of world which we have developed for ourselves and they condemn it as exploitative and ruthless, as myopically materialistic, constructed upon too narrow a foundation.

W.B. Yeats certainly believed that we had taken a wrong turn. However, he also optimistically believed that we were about to find our way back to the central highway and he devoted his life to helping us do so.

For Yeats and for Kathleen Raine, the sages who can teach us a knowledge of another kind are the great poets and visionaries whose wisdom has been harvested in the so-called sacred books from all spiritual traditions. For these two twentieth-century protagonists of an alternative world, William Blake (1757–1827) was such a prophet:

> Who beat upon the wall
> Till Truth obeyed his call[4]

The difficulty is that many people regard William Blake as insane and Yeats as not much better. Kathleen Raine is dismissed by this widespread constituency as a lesser poet in her dotage, or a semi-religious quack.

Listen to John Carey, Merton Professor at Oxford University and chair of the Man Booker prize for 2004, here reviewing the first volume of Roy Foster's biography[5] of W.B. Yeats: 'Was he, you find yourself blasphemously wondering, really that intelligent?' and he lists the usual proofs of intellectual backwardness: 'He was substandard at school … He never learnt to spell: even as a grown man, simple monosyllables foxed him … His gullibility was fathomless. Mysticism and magic, to which he was introduced by the half-batty George Russell, occupied much of his waking and sleeping life. He believed he conversed with old Celtic gods and a copious ragbag of other supernaturals.'[6]

Such critics may or may not believe that we have taken a major detour from the path of Truth, but they certainly do not regard Yeats as a trustworthy guide to a better path, and such critics hold the high ground in influential academic circles.

Yeats wrote in his introduction to Lady Gregory's *Gods and Fighting Men* (1904), 'Children at play, at being great and wonderful people' are the true reality of what we are and what we should become. 'Mankind as a whole had a like dream once; everybody and nobody built up the dream bit by bit and the story-tellers are there to make us remember.' But the children of the twentieth century had put away these ambitions and for one reason or another we simply grew into ordinary men and women. How did this happen?

In his letters Yeats dated our defection, our detour from the true heritage opened for us by imagination and religion, to the seventeenth century. In 1926 he wrote to Sturge Moore, 'As A.N. Whitehead puts it: "The seventeenth century produced a scheme of scientific thought framed by mathematicians for the use of mathematicians."'[7]

We are symbolic animals. Everything we understand or comprehend is received by us symbolically. If I ask you to draw a tree and if I draw one myself, both our attempts will be different almost to the point of contradiction. How can both these drawings represent the same thing? And yet we understand both to be trees. I use a triangular form, you use a circular one to describe the reality which both of us recognise as trees in the world around us. Yet neither of our representations look anything like any trees we have ever seen in our lives. They don't look like each other and they don't look like what they are meant to represent, yet they are symbols which we can both recognise (see p. 67). And that is the way our heads work. We cannot receive or transmit images in any other way.

This applies to all my day-to-day dealings of whatever kind. If I go into a shop and ask for a hat, the person behind the counter can retire to the store behind and return with a busby or a sombrero. I can tell him that the busby is too tall, too heavy and too difficult to put on my head; that the sombrero is too wide, too flat and too flimsy. He makes a symbolic calculation in his mind. He doesn't, and he cannot, pass the actual bearskin busby or the real felt or straw sombrero through the space in his head, he instead reproduces an image of these, based upon shorthand geometrical sketches which both he and I are constantly flashing through our minds as we negotiate, and he then goes back into the store and returns with a bowler or a Homburg which seem to be a compromise in terms of size, shape, texture and design. In other words he has taken the geometrical outline of the tall overweight busby, removed its material trappings and reduced it to an abstract sketch of itself and then halved and reduced it to double the height of the sombrero without the circular trappings. All of which are the kind of geometrical symbolism which automatically goes on in our heads every minute of our daily lives. Geometry is, in this way, the most natural and fluent symbolism of the mind.

An equivalent is true when we are counting. If we didn't have fingers it is unlikely that we would have learned to count in the way we do. A finger is *digitus* in Latin so it becomes the most primitive form of digital calculation. As we have ten fingers and the Latin for ten is *decimus* we automatically engage in 'decimal' systems until we run out of fingers and have to start again. Many ancient languages use the word 'jump' for the number six to remind themselves to pass from the left hand to the right once they reach the number five.

$5 + 5 = 10$.

We're all pretty competent as far as that goes. But

$5 \times 5 = 5+5+5+5+5$.

That switch of combined symbolism (the numbers on the one hand and the x and + on the other) is confounding even if you use your toes (also *digitus* in Latin) as well. You have to find ways of compressing. Symbols are compressed versions of larger realities.

> 'What's the first thing you'd do if you won the lotto?'
> 'I'd count it.'

Okay, but you'll need a more sophisticated form of calculation than your two hands and two feet once the sum goes over the million. Mathematics supplies such a calculating symbolism. Science also seeks to reduce the world of experience to the most abstract and universally applicable formulae. From the seventeenth century this one form of symbolism, the mathematical and scientific, was regarded as the only one. Other symbolic forms were obsolete. They led up to this enlightened era and from now on the world could be explored, understood and conquered by science and technology.

This is a very plausible explanation of how we have become as narrowminded as we are, but in my view it is not radical or extensive enough. We have to go back further than that to explain our present entrapment. To do this I shall be relying heavily upon the people who best explained it to me.[8] *Homo Sapiens,* the technical term for the human species, has been on earth perhaps fifty thousand years. Writing, in the strict sense of the word, the technology which has shaped and powered the intellectual activity of modern man, was a very late development in human history. The first script, or true writing, that we know, was developed among the Sumerians in Mesopotamia about 3500 BCE.

When does a footprint or a deposit of faeces or urine (used by many species of animals for communication) become 'writing'? … when a coded system of visible marks was invented whereby a writer could determine the exact words that the reader would generate from the text … so that the exquisitely intricate structures and references evolved in sound can be visibly recorded exactly in their specific complexity. Writing in this ordinary sense was and is the most momentous of all human technological inventions. Notches on sticks and other *aides-mémoire* lead up to writing, but they do not restructure the human lifeworld as true writing does (Ong 83–85).

The shapes of letters in most languages are derived from common forms in nature. Letters and symbols in Chinese, Latin, Persian and all ninety-seven of the other writing systems have shapes that humans are good at seeing. The figures we use in symbolic systems seem to be selected because they are easy to see.

> The Greeks did something of major psychological importance when they developed the first alphabet complete with vowels … abstractly analysing the elusive world of sound into visual equivalents … democratising and internationalising … This completely phonetic

alphabet favours left-hemisphere activity in the brain, and thus fosters abstract, analytic thought. Sound exists only when it is going out of existence. The alphabet represents sound itself as a thing. Although perhaps derived from pictograms it has lost all connection with things as things. (Ong 91–92)

When we talk about the 'the technology of writing' we need to explain ourselves. Nowadays 'techology' is thought of in terms of computers and complicated machinery of various kinds. We could be excused if we thought of the first forms of writing as somehow pre-technological. And yet writing has always required quite sophisticated equipment and a series of tools which were necessary for the performance of this highly unnatural task. Even today many of us carry a 'pen knife', without recognising that the name implies an instrument for sharpening goose quills. All writing further required some kind of ink with a portable and impermeable holder, usually a hollow bovine inkhorn. Paper or parchment, often made from cowskins, was required. What we now take for granted as paper was first manufactured in China in the second century BCE and sold by Arabs to the Middle East by the eighth century of the Christian era. Paper was first manufactured in Europe only in the twelfth century (Ong 95).

Now the point of emphasising the technological dimensions of the written word from the very beginning is also to stress the connection and the continuity between writing, printing and, eventually, computers. Of these three immensely influential technologies, writing was by far the most drastic. It initiated what print and computers only continued, 'the reduction of dynamic sound to quiescent space' (Ong 82). Reading and writing detach and isolate us: 'Writing is a solipsistic operation.' Sight isolates, sound incorporates. Vision comes to a human being from one direction at a time: to look at a room or a landscape, I must move my eyes around from one part to another. When I hear, however, I gather sound simultaneously from every direction at once: I am at the centre of my auditory world, which envelops me (Ong 72). For oral cultures, the cosmos is an ongoing event with people at its centre. Only after print and the extensive experience with maps that print implemented would human beings, when they thought about the cosmos or universe or 'world', think primarily of something laid out before their eyes, as in a modern printed atlas, a vast surface or assemblage of surfaces (vision presents surfaces) ready to be 'explored' (Ong 37).

In Western European philosophy we were introduced by Auguste Comte to the idea that human intelligence had developed from a primitive mythic stage, through a medieval metaphysical stage, right up to the scientific rationalism which has so marked and transformed our world. This development was linear and rendered all stages that preceded it obsolete. 'Civilised' peoples have always contrasted themselves with 'primitive' or 'savage' peoples. One of the pivotal anthropological works of recent decades is Claude Lévi-Strauss's *La Pensée Sauvage* (1962). Earlier works of Lucien Lévy-Bruhl, *Les Fonctions mentales dans les sociétés inférieures* (1910) and *La Mentalité Primitive* (1923) all show in their titles the condescending approach to the kind of peoples here involved.

There is no such evolutionary progress in a linear module, which casts off the previous in an advance towards the present, as a rocket might detach itself from the parts that launch it. Mythic intelligence is an essential kind of human understanding and it is to our great impoverishment that our educational systems and our academic leaders treat it with such contempt.

It was only much later that I read the four volumes of Ernst Cassirer's *The Philosophy of Symbolic Forms*[9] which vindicated all aspects of my early life on Knockfierna and explained how 'the mythical intuition of space' occupies 'a kind of middle position between the space of sense perception and the space of pure cognition, that is, geometry.' He explained with clarity that the space of perception, which is the space of vision, of touch, of smell, of taste, of hearing, is not the same as the space of pure mathematics, 'that there is indeed a thoroughgoing divergence between the two.' In fact mathematical or geometrical, call it 'metric', space cannot be derived from sensory space 'in an unbroken logical sequence.' On the contrary, the first-hand, sensory experience and perception of life on Knockfierna has to be denied in order to reach the metric space of geometry and mathematics. 'We require a peculiar reversal of perspective, a *negation* of what seems immediately given in sensory perception, before we can arrive at the "logical space" of pure mathematics.' Geometry and mathematics invent a space which is homogenous, 'which is never given space, but space produced by construction.' The geometrical concept of homogeneity can be expressed by the postulate that from every point in space it must be possible to draw similar figures in all directions and magnitudes. As I am sitting in the ringfort on the side of Knockfierna it must be possible to calculate my position from every side in the same way. But nowhere in the space of lived reality can such homogeneity be achieved. Visual space and tactile space have their own 'mode' and 'value'. In sensory space and in mythical space no 'here' and 'there' is merely a here and there, a term in a universal relation. Before/behind, above/below, right/left, are all different and 'anisotropic'. What Cassirer demonstrates is that 'mythical space' is closely related to the space of sensory perception and opposed to the logical space of geometry. In the first two every point and every element has a tonality of its own and a 'special distinguishing character' which cannot be described in general terms but must be immediately experienced as it is for what it is. 'In contrast to the homogeneity which prevails in the conceptual space of geometry every position and direction in mythical space is endowed as it were with a particular accent.'[10] And this form of consciousness, this kind of knowledge, has every right to exist, to be cultivated, promoted and valorised, just as much as the mathematical and geometrical. So it is not a question of denying the value of mathematical and scientific knowledge. It is rather a question of reinstating another kind of knowledge which is equally important and *sui generis*. The important fact to recognise is that for so many years this other kind of knowledge has been undermined if not suppressed.

It is difficult for us to step outside the spaceship and recognise just how programmed we are. Much in the same way that we recognise the overwhelming extent to which we are dependent upon electricity only when there is a power cut, we have to exercise our imagination almost violently to recognise the extent to which we are automised clones of an infrastructural grid called 'common sense'. We are able to symbolise mythically, artistically, religiously, but these faculties are erased by our learning only the three Rs.

People of Western Europe in the twentieth century were not only able to read and write more or less instinctively, they translated everything that presented itself to them into this narrow network. We *read* music, art, cinema, life and love. Every time we enter an art gallery we don't look at the pictures, we read the little label posted at the side. Faced by an abstract painting of white on white we are totally bemused until we read the caption which says: 'picture of an aeroplane gone out of sight.' Now we understand perfectly. Everything we do must be a story, an alphabet, a grammar, a plot, a chapter, a closed book, a bestseller. We read and write our lives. My diary is my day translated into coherent literacy.

From four years of age all children are condemned to a bookish, commercial education. Recent decisions of the United Nations propose to inflict this myopia on all children of the world in the name of equality of opportunity and universal human rights.

Our hypnosis here does not simply start in the seventeenth century. It goes right back to the Middle Ages. For well over a thousand years we were subjected to a debilitating and diminishing educational system. Ong dates this to a time in Europe when 'High Latin' which was never a 'mother tongue' (taught by one's mother) became for many generations of Europeans their only access to so-called higher education. Obviously Latin was once a spoken language but it became a 'school language', completely controlled by writing, once it ceased to be a vernacular tongue for those who used it. It became the *lingua franca* of the universities based in academia and suffusing an exclusively male environment.

> For well over a thousand years [Latin] was sex-linked, a language written and spoken only by males, learned outside the home in a tribal setting which was in effect a male puberty rite setting, complete with physical punishment and other kinds of deliberately imposed hardships. It had no direct connection with anyone's unconscious of the sort that mother tongues, learned in infancy, always have. Devoid of baby-talk, insulated from the earliest life of childhood where language has its deepest psychic roots, a first language to none of its users, pronounced across Europe in often mutually unintelligible ways but always written the same way, Learned Latin was a striking exemplification of the power of writing for isolating discourse and of the unparalleled productivity of such isolation … making possible the exquisitely abstract world of medieval scholasticism and of the new mathematical modern science which followed on the scholastic experience. Without Learned Latin, it appears that modern science would have got under way with greater difficulty, if it had got under way at all. Modern science grew in Latin soil, for philosophers and scientists through the time of Sir

Isaac Newton commonly both wrote and did their abstract thinking in Latin. (Ong 113–114)

Not only did the so-called 'three Rs' come from such a mono-symbolic bias, but the catechism of Catholic doctrine also grew from this soil. It was a simplified synopsis of medieval scholasticism. Most of our education from the age of four is at a third remove from the reality which we perceive around us. Between the metric space of mathematics and physics and the topological space of our childhood world there are several symbolic variations to which we have access as children and which we ignore and abandon to our impoverishment.

Music, art, myth are all symbolic systems or structures which allow us to process the subtle fashion by which the world attaches itself to the delicate sprockets of our sensibility and our psyche. 'The mythical consciousness of space is interwoven with the sphere of subjective feeling', Cassirer tells us. This makes it hugely important for our eventual integration because mathematics and physics, by the nature of their operative efficacity, are obliged to dissociate completely from the subjective world of feeling. This means that 'the facts of physics are not on the same footing with the facts of history because they rest on entirely different presuppositions and intellectual procedures.' We take three important steps towards the third remove from reality as we live it in our daily lives. Mythical 'expressive space' is transformed into 'representative space' and this in turn is transformed by the thinking of physics which 'effects the final step to pure "significative space".'[11] It is through such a transposition, Cassirer explains, 'that the concept of temperature takes form from the mere sensation of heat, the concept of pressure from mere tactile and muscular sensation.'[12] Education which neglects these intermediary symbolic stages between the world of sensation and the world of the three Rs is myopic and unbalanced.

Harry Potter
and the Three Rs

More than half the children in the United Kingdom name one of the Harry Potter stories in their three favourite books. Joanne Kathleen Rowling (pronounced 'rolling') is certainly living up to her name at the moment. In 2003, at the age of thirty-nine, she was named the world's highest-paid author. Once an unemployed single mother, she is now ranked at number 552 out of a record number of five hundred and eighty-seven billionaires in the Forbes list of 2004. In October 2005, her literary agent announced that the boy wizard series had sold more than three hundred million copies worldwide. The six books published in the series so far have been translated into sixty-three languages. The first four have also been made into blockbuster movies.

Many conservative Christian parents refuse to allow their children to read the Potter stories because they contend that these have too much evil and darkness in them and therefore promote witchcraft and wickedness. Pastor Jack Brock of Christ Community Church in Alamogordo, New Mexico, had a holy bonfire on the Sunday after Christmas 2001, in which he burnt the Potter books publicly as 'an abomination to God and to me'. Richard Abanes in *Harry Potter and The Bible*, shows a direct link with 'current paganism' and the practice of witchcraft, as well as ties to occult and new-age philosophy. Connie Neal's book *What's a Christian to do with Harry Potter?* has a chapter entitled: 'What would Jesus do with Harry Potter?'

The Potter mythology, as well as having classical allusions (described by Elizabeth Schafer in *Exploring Harry Potter*) is also steeped in the Christian tradition which spawned both the author and her hero.[1]

> The only newness about Rowling's fictional world is the freshness with which she treats old themes and invents new ones. The world of magic and miracle has been around for a long, long time, and is an intrinsic part of the Judeo-Christian heritage, whatever explanations conservative Christians may wish to offer for it.

The promotional literature reads

> Harry Potter has never been the star of a Quidditch team, scoring points while riding a broom far above the ground. He knows no spells, has never helped to hatch a dragon, and has never worn a cloak of invisibility. All he knows is a miserable life with the Dursleys, his horrible aunt and uncle, and their abominable son, Dudley – a great big swollen spoiled bully. Harry's room is a tiny closet at the foot of the stairs, and he hasn't had a birthday party in eleven years. But all that is about to change when a mysterious letter arrives by an owl messenger: a letter with an invitation to an incredible place that Harry – and anyone who reads about him – will find unforgettable.

J.K. Rowling has a relationship with our children, and indeed with ourselves as children, which we should envy and encourage. Far from trying to stop the lights we should be helping them to burn more brightly. She is doing more for imagination than any other single force in our thoroughly bleak and businesslike century.

The truth is that every one of us who has suffered through so-called 'free' education in Western Europe during the twentieth century is Harry Potter. Imagination was given no birthday party and had its tiny little room under the stairs. We have been educated out of myth and magic. We have had our capacity to symbolise erased from the desktop of our internal computers.

The three Rs became the fundamental educational currency in the West. They also became the criteria for 'intelligence' measured by specifically narrow IQ tests designed by the perpetrators of the official system. Only those who have fallen between the bars of the grid know the extent to which they are marginalised and deprived by illiteracy. We imagine that reading and writing are natural to us, whereas, in fact, they must be two of the most unnatural activities ever undertaken by creatures on this planet. In themselves they are, of course, invaluable skills which introduce us to a world of possibility. On their own, as substitutes for all other kinds of understanding and expression, they are debilitating.

Hybrids

The second school I went to was Glenstal Abbey about fifty kilometres away from my home. I went at the age of twelve and remained there – apart from a series of absences which lasted in toto not more than a decade – for the next fifty years. The reason why you go somewhere is rarely the reason why you stay. I am aware that one of the purposes of having a school in the monastery was to ensure the survival of the species. Individual boys were approached by monks whom they admired and told that following lengthy consultations with the heavenly hierarchy they were being considered for entry to the novitiate. Not all the boys were regarded as worthy of such canvassing but I was told by at least three different monks that my name was being mentioned in high places. Half of me was flattered that I should be discussed in the heavenly courts; the other half was horrified. I had always been interested in, and deeply aware of, God but most of my conversations had been conducted on Knockfierna. I began to understand that it was impossible to be a mystic on a mountainside. I had to find a place.

Glenstal is a place. The name identifies the ghost of a male horse seen galloping through the archway of the castle. The 'glen of the stallion' has been a hybrid place from its beginnings. Geographically and historically anomalous, it is situated in the countryside of south-east Limerick. Its landscape is dominated by a nineteenth-century Norman castle pretending to be built in the twelfth century. Sir Charles Barrington selected the site so that each room on the south side of the castle would have a view of the Galtee mountains. He constructed five artificial lakes around the castle to add the element of water to this landscape. The stone tower overlooking a panoramic vista, from the river Shannon on the east to the Galtee mountains in the south, bears the name of the architect, Billy Barden, and the date of completion, 1138, is carved on the inner side of the tower beneath the parapet. Around the second number '1' a silhouetted figure of eight is superimposed to soften the lie and circumlocute the truth. The mock castle appeared in the early nineteenth century. It was apparently built on the model of Windsor Castle outside London. Stone statues of Eleanor of Aquitaine and Henry II of France guard the front door to remind those who enter that they are now on planter land: this is Protestant territory inside a predominantly Catholic country and 'there is some corner of a foreign field/that is forever England'. The grounds were designed as an earthly paradise. These gardens have since grown into a jungle and the ornamental rhododendrons designed as shrubs have escalated into colourful forests. The place has reverted to 'Irishry' by default.

Tragic circumstances of history caused the estate to change hands. The Barrington daughter, Winnie, was shot and killed by mistake by the IRA who had ambushed her lover, a major in the British Army stationed in Tipperary at that time. The family moved back to England and their beautiful castle and estate became a Benedictine monastery in 1927. What was once a two-dimensional anomaly now inhabited at least four dimensions. Where two countries and two times had been cleverly juxtaposed in one place, heaven was to combine with earth, time with eternity, in one place at every moment of each day. 'I don't know what you monks are going to do when you get to heaven,' visitors have said, 'and you find that you were already there!' The place had always been accustomed to ambidexterity, now it would have to stretch this potential to the limits.

The castle which the monks inherited was a fortress on a mountain. Its round towers, slit windows and stone facades spelt defensiveness. Its purpose was to keep out the world and it was built to enclose its members in a circle of protected insulation. The monks put the word *'pax'* over the portcullis to increase the paradox. A massive cannon was found in the lake and was mounted with wheels on the terrace facing the front avenue. Every time the monks held an ecumenical meeting at the abbey they seemed to photograph themselves with their guests sitting beside this cannon. They thought it would be a picturesque setting for the newspapers. They failed to register the irony. The day after the cannon was erected the guards arrived from the village asking whether it had a licence. The price to pay for a licence is gauged by the weight of the firearm. This one weighed in tonnes. Shortly after the summons the picturesque weapon of mass destruction was decommissioned.

I moved to this location from my birth place at the age of twelve. It has become for me a different kind of home. A poem by Francis Thompson (1859–1907), who died in the year my parents were born, describes the entrapment. 'The Hound of Heaven' is based upon Psalm 138 which the monks sing every Thursday at vespers:

> I fled him, down the nights and down the days;
> I fled him, down the arches of the years
> I fled him down the labyrinthine ways
> Of my own mind.
>
> (For, though I knew His love Who followèd,
> Yet was I sore adread
> Lest, having Him, I must have naught beside.)

* * *

My grandfather like Lord Barrington was a great lover of trees. One tree on the front avenue of our home, which I associate particularly with an awareness of the presence of God in my early life, was a peculiar one. It was a common beech tree onto which my grandfather had grafted a fern-leaved beech. By the time I was standing under it, the two different trees had grown together to an equal height while sharing the same trunk. It was a hybrid tree which botanists found worthy of notice. Both Glenstal itself, and my move there in 1956, have much in common with this twinned beech.

The biggest tree I can remember in my home was in front of the house and beside an ornamental lake. It was a Turkish oak planted by my grandfather and was as wide as it was tall. It represented the strength and sturdiness of my father's family in that place. When I made profession in the monastery here in 1965 my father brought me a seedling from that tree which I planted beside the chapel lake. Across the lake from where this seedling was planted there is a Californian redwood tree which, until it was hit by lighting and the top of it removed, was the tallest sequoia this side of the Atlantic. Sir Charles Barrington, another great lover of trees, went to America with his friend Douglas, after whom the fir is named, and brought back many specimens which he planted in Glenstal. There is a bridge between these two trees which joins my mother's country, America, to my father's house. In the meantime, the original Turkish oak in my home place was blown down in a storm. No trace of it remains.

When I was two years in the monastery I was thinking of leaving. I wrote to my mother and she sent me some lines from the same Francis Thompson:

> Leave thy father, leave thy mother
> And thy brother;
> Leave the black tents of thy tribe apart!

Am I not thy father and thy brother,
And thy mother?
And thou – what needest with thy tribe's black tents
Who hast the red pavilion of my heart?

The turkish oak beside the chapel lake became my red pavilion. The bridge between the two also joins, at two different levels, a graveyard, a seventeenth-century terraced garden, and a deep ravine which dates back to the ice age, preserving rare species of botanical growth (see p. 68). The crossroads here have, therefore, four compartments and two dimensions: the garden, the glen, the graveyard and the gateway.

The graveyard has a picturesque wall complete with creaking gate framed somewhat exotically by yew trees, symbols for the Celts of eternal life (see p. 68). It is an ideal scene for Gothic horror movies. A writer of such tales, Sheridan LeFanu (1814–1873), lived in this area and wrote *The House by the Churchyard* in 1864, among other tales of mystery and imagination. The Ilchester oak at the end of the front avenue certainly inspired some love scenes in his stories. Trees speak a language of their own as well as scraping the surface of the sky.

The garden, the glen, the graveyard and the greenery make up the four elements of the crossroads plus the swinging of the door. Geography leads through to another garden on the strength of that particular hinge. The cross, as in every crossroads, is the major symbol of Christianity and this particular combination describes the way in which Christianity has become incarnate in this place. Not a cross as an instrument of torture; rather as a way upward and forward. Christ hoisting humanity to another, a higher, a hybrid dimension. The bridge is large with massive arches describing length and breadth, height and depth. It was built with four stone arches but when looked at from the footpath at the lowest point of the lake beneath, appears to have only three. The fourth is completely obscured by trees and vegetation, yet the bridge looks perfectly symmetrical and natural. The fourth dimension needs to be revealed.

These dimensions are replicated in the surrounding geography. Steps lead abruptly from the top of a cliff on the left hand side of the crossroads to the depths of the ice-age crevice until they reach a mass-rock where people celebrated their faith in Penal times. This is also the rock on which our church is built, the bedrock of who we really are. We reach it by going down those steps each in our own lives. The steps of humility are ones which lead us down to the depths of the earth. It takes another kind of time. The same word in Latin, *humus*, augurs both – earth and humility.

The seventeenth-century walled garden beyond the stone bridge over the chapel lake is built in old red sandstone of the Munster variety which gives it a warm, almost human glow. (Murroe, the village beside, means 'the red plain' in Irish). Sown into the crevices of these stately garden walls by the creator of this terraced tattoo, in an otherwise wild and rugged landscape, are small white daisies which cling to the rock. The gardeners had chosen these specifically, with a pink fleck on the tip of each petal, to pick out the colour of the stone. Such is the pink fleck of a variety of human life which has turned this natural setting into a supernatural trampoline. This has only emerged in very recent memory: a mere seventy-five years of what must be a history of hundreds of years if measured by the trees, thousands of years if counted in the rocks, millions of years in meteors buried beneath this earth.

I am trying to describe another kind of space: sacred space, sacramental space. Such space can happen in any particular place we inhabit at any particular moment in time, even in hospital or in prison. A Russian soldier, condemned to death by being buried alive, was in a state of panic as the coffin doors were being closed about him. He asked to have his favourite icon buried with him. When it was put into his hand he held his peace.

Climbing mountains has often been a symbol of spiritual ascent, movement from one kind of place to another. Mount Olympus and Mount Parnassus were dwelling places of the gods for the ancient Greeks. The Judeo-Christian tradition is encrusted with mountains where conversations with God have taken place: Ararat, Calvary, Carmel, Hermon, Horeb, Mizar, Nebo, Olivet, Sinai, Sion, Thabor, Zion. Of these, Sinai and Thabor have taken pride of place. In the Christian tradition Thabor, the mountain of the Transfiguration, has come to represent the fulfilment of the Hebrew conversation with God. Sinai and Thabor symbolise the journey from one holy mountain to the other: the covenant of the law to the communion of love. Christianity embraced such symbolism from its beginnings.

Philo in the first century through Gregory of Nyssa and the pseudo-Dionysios the Areopagite depicted Sinai as exemplifying the spiritual life of Moses and his mystical ascent towards God. Later, Mount Thabor, where the Transfiguration of Jesus Christ took place, became the quintessential Christian mountain. Three apostles were present when Jesus was revealed in glory and with him on this mountain were Moses and Elijah representing the Law and the prophets of the earlier covenant. For Christians the significance of Mount Thabor is not only the revelation of the glory which has become our inheritance as brothers and sisters of Jesus Christ, but it is the transfiguration of an earlier experience of God on another mountain, and fulfilment of its promise. Such a transfiguration and transposition is my own experience as I moved from Knockfierna and the Eiger Mountain to the monastery at Glenstal Abbey.

Early iconography, the earliest to have survived from the Monastery of St Catherine on Mount Sinai, for instance, gives a minimalist depiction of the mountain of Transfiguration, which appears flat and low. In the ninth and tenth centuries the mountain in such iconography becomes almost disproportionately exaggerated, taking up the largest area of the picture and appearing as vast and tall. Art has preceded and outstripped the much later theological emphasis on the importance of the mountain as the space and place of communion with the divine: art has depicted iconographically and symbolically what was only put in writing some centuries later. Art, like the divine evangelist, reaches the place of resurrection first.

Each of us must find our own symbols and our own mythology: the symbols which open to us the door to another world and the myth which expresses our journey to and through such openings. My own personal story has been that of *The Count of Monte Cristo*, a very old story, written in 1844 by Alexander Dumas. The story tells of a very young man, Edmund Dantes, who, on the day of his promotion to captain of a ship and of his marriage to his girlfriend, Mercedes, is accused of treason and thrown into a dungeon in the Château d'If, an infamous French prison on an island off the coast of Marseilles. Here he is left to languish in solitary confinement. Another prisoner, an old priest, who is trying to escape from this prison by tunneling his way towards the outer walls, happens, by chance, to find his way to Dantes's cell and they decide to try to escape together. The priest has a secret map which leads to a vast treasure trove on the island of Monte Cristo. During their time together the priest educates the young man and explains how to read the map and find the treasure on the distant island. The priest dies before either of them escape and, as was the custom in this island prison, his dead body is wrapped in a sack, attached to a ball and chain, and thrown into the ocean. However, the younger man has managed to substitute himself for the dead body of the older priest, and is the one who is thrown over the parapet into the sea. He swims ashore and is soon on his way to Monte Cristo with the map as guide. Having found the treasure, he returns to Paris with a new identity as The Count of Monte

Cristo. He begins to take revenge on those who accused him falsely and had him condemned to life imprisonment.

The story is an old one which has reemerged in several guises. It is the basis for other stories, films and plays, which achieve their popularity because of the archetypal structure and plot. Every person on this planet has, at some time or other, been condemned to a situation or a lifestyle which is death to what they enjoyed previously: ejection from the womb, the abrupt end to childhood, illness, incarceration, retirement; any or all of these can be mirror images of the Monte Cristo story.

In my own case, it was the decision to enter a monastery, where the technical word for your room is your 'cell' in which, when you arrive, there is nothing but a bed, a chair and a table, and where the kindly novice-master asks you, without the slightest hint of irony: 'Have you got everything you need?' The monastery at Glenstal Abbey was originally built as an eleventh-century Norman castle and it resembles in profile the Château d'If (see p. 69). The monk is meant to give up everything he has, everything he could be, in the workaday world. It is a grim prospect on the first days of transmigration. However, after a certain length of time the mountain climb begins and the transfiguration takes place. The life inside the walls has its own tradition and this means a 'handing on' of a secret map which leads to a treasure trove. The result is escape from the prison, sufficient acquaintance with the map to allow you to find the treasure, which in turn makes of you a count or countess. The word comes from the Latin *'comes'* and derives from its accusative form *'comitem'* meaning companion and, later, 'companion of the king or emperor'. Monte Cristo means 'the mountain of Christ'. And so the transfiguration is complete, as is the symbol. Personal friends of Christ (*comites*), 'impersoned' embodiments of the Holy Spirit, become dwellers on his holy mountain (*Monte Cristo*), a world resurrected by divine energy, visible, tangible and available through a variety of escutcheoned doors.

A monastery should be such a space. It should introduce us also to another kind of time. It does so mostly through music of various kinds which breaks up the monotony of chronological time and inserts a syncopated rhythm.

The most obvious symbol of such two-timing is the bell. A bell is not a natural phenomenon, it has to be cast. This makes it a symbol par excellence because in Greek, in which the word originates, 'sym' means 'together' and 'balein' means 'thrown or cast together'. Bells are cast by many hands. In Russia bells were believed to address the deity directly. Russian monks constructed enormous ones to add strength to prayer. The world's largest bell was made in Russia and it weighs 200 tons. Big Ben in London weighs only 13 tons by comparison. The oldest surviving bell, since human beings began to cast metal, came from Babylon five thousand years ago. In Europe the making of bells was a monastic craft, the particular art-form of the monks. It was that magical mixture of tin and copper which turned into bronze and then was able to produce a sonorous tone.

Like pottery, the making was fraught with potential disaster: air bubbles could form as the metal solidified which would create pockets of weakness. A cracked bell became synonymous with something or someone essentially flawed. Our language has taken up the symbolism. Alarm bells, cow bells, dinner bells, sleigh bells, sound as a bell, clear as a bell. We name flowers Canterbury bells, bluebells. 'The curfew tolls the knell of passing day.' The bell strikes out the passing hours. The bell is bisexual and comprises a vulva with a phallus that rings out the *mysterium coniunctionis* – sacred marriage of opposites, the symbol par excellence.

And that is what a monastery should be: a place where bells are cast, beautiful pottery made. Except that the casting and the throwing are done by and with human beings. A monastery is an art studio for humanity.

Even here in this life we are invited to become hybrid creatures, fully paid-up members of the Blessed Trinity, as well as ordinary human beings. We are handed the possibility of living the life of resurrection as of now. It is a decision we can make, a reality we can accomplish at each moment of our day, remembering who we are and what we are called to be. Of course we forget and we slump back into the biological rhythm of life which is natural to us, the horizontal line of what T.S. Eliot calls: birth, copulation and death. Resurrection is an upward movement. It says that we are more than biology. We can switch over to an alternative energy which is everlasting. This changes the time and space scenario of our everyday lives. We transfigure the twenty-four hours of the day into the day of resurrection, *Hodie*, the last day, forever. And we change our location, we bilocate. Eternity enters the grain of sand and infinity the wild creatures that we are.

Part Two:

Art

Art

Art was there before the rest of us arrived at such conclusions. In earlier times inner vision presented itself in a coherent language of mythology or religion. These were the *lingua franca* or common parlance of those who dwelt on this planet. What we call 'modern art' is the logical outcome of the Renaissance. During that period of rebirth our minds underwent a radical change. We might say that we went from extraversion to introversion. The exploration of the outer world was partnered by a new exploration of the inner world, the subjective world. And this was an exploration that could not depend on the old map of religion. And now neither mythology nor religion are capable of moving the people of our contemporary world. That is why we have to depend once again upon the artist. If an artist is a person of genius, he or she can find eternity and infinity, God and all his works, within his- or herself, and can externalise these for the rest of us. This is why, in times when both politics and religion are found wanting, we have to rely on artists.

In painting and literature the term 'symbolist' has a technical meaning which describes a movement in these arts dating from the end of the nineteenth century. The name came from an article in the literary supplement of *Le Figaro* in France on the 18 September 1886, in which Jean Moréas tried to describe the trend being established in recent French poetry: 'Symbolic poetry attempts to clothe the Idea in a perceptible form which, though not itself the poem's goal, serves to express the Idea to which it remains subordinate.' The practictioners liked the label and adopted it. Their poetry was indeed an attempt to make present a reality which would otherwise remain inexpressible. The function of the symbol was to express what is absent, otherwordly, transcendental. Obviously, symbolism was not born in 1886 but a group of artists who had appeared in France at least twenty years before that date and who were applying the principles articulated by Morés came together under this umbrella. They were all opposed to the so-called progress of nineteenth-century civilisation which had banished all reality outside the expressible order of scientific observation. Jules Laforgue banned any world other than this one, and famously requested infinity to present its papers. Reality had no time for dreamers and poetry lent no wings to sordid daytime. The symbol at the heart of symbolism stood opposed to the limited 'reality' of this age.

At the end of the nineteenth century, while science and so-called 'positivism' were triumphantly announcing a brave new world founded on reason and technology, some dissenters were aware of the heavy losses involved. They sought to express an indefinable quality which had been buried in the previous cultural system of religion and mythology, the world-view of their ancestors. Symbolists took a melancholy view of the new vista and hankered for all the hidden values and meanings which were contained in the old emblematic order. They regretted being born into a dying world of the opulent past and the emergence of a cheap and one-dimensional substitute. They spoke of the moon rather than the sun, and celebrated Autumn more than springtime. Symbolist origins in France bespoke a disillusioned royalist and Catholic remnant of an older medieval and European order. Whereas the Romantic movement, as a parallel reaction against the scientific and industrialist ethos of the time, was rooted in the Protestant mentality of Germany and developed into an almost mystical connection with nature, symbolism was born of a Catholic mentality in France, Belgium, Austria and parts of Germany. For all its ambiguity, the cross, as a central symbol of this movement, represented not so much any religious affiliation as a sign of a world which acknowledged more than one plane of reality.[1] Connected with this very specific and reactionary movement, symbolism became tainted with conservative, nostalgic and overblown tendencies. It was around this time also that the world of surrealism was invoked. It too was positing some dimension of reality other than the visible and the vulgar ever-present before our eyes.

The Day
the Earth Moved

There was a time when symbolism was the norm. Hans Holbein the Younger (1497–1543) was born in Augsburg, Bavaria, where his father, who first taught him, was also an artist. In 1515 he went to Basel, in Switzerland, with his brother, Ambrosius. The year he arrived was the fiftieth anniversary of the first Swiss printing press. Although, as we have already noted, printing was first conceived and developed in China and Korea, printing did not develop in Europe until the mid-fifteenth century. Apparently, the oldest printed book using woodblock technique was a Korean Buddhist scripture, dating back to 751 CE, and the oldest surviving book using such block printing is the Chinese *Diamond Sutra*, which dates from 868 CE. Such movable type metal printing presses were invented in Korea during the Goryeo Dynasty, two hundred and sixteen years ahead of Gutenberg who has been hailed as their European inventor in 1450.

However, all such technology was new to Europe and inspired many artists of genius to use it as an expressive medium. Holbein was associated early on with these Basel publishers and their circle, most particularly the famous Dutch humanist Desiderius Erasmus, who asked the young artist to illustrate his satirical book, *Encomium Moriae* (In Praise of Folly). Holbein's first major portrait of Erasmus (1523, Louvre, Paris) shows the humanist scholar as physically withdrawn from the world, sitting at his desk engaged in his voluminous European correspondence. Writing was his way of communicating with the universe around him. These were the important years when the technology of writing developed into the technology of printing, when the Renaissance evolved into the scientific revolution, when the religion of the Middle Ages underwent the Reformation. Holbein, as one of the greatest and most accurate depictors of reality, was on hand to record these transitional moments for posterity. He was recognised as a great artist by most of the patrons who mattered among his contemporaries, but he increased his fame and his worldwide recognition when he illustrated one of the most influential books to avail of the new technology: Martin Luther's German translation of the Bible.

While in Basel, Holbein had also been active in designing woodcuts for title pages and book illustrations. His most famous work in this area is a series of forty-one scenes designed by him and cut by another artist between 1523 and 1526 but not published until 1538, illustrating the medieval allegorical concept of the dance of death. One of these woodcuts is called *The Escutcheon of Death*. This too would prove to be a clairvoyant depiction of another symbolic cataclysm of this time: the bubonic plague, as reoccurrence of the Black Death, which decimated much of Europe from the middle of the fourteenth century and which in the end claimed Holbein's life.

In the year of Holbein's death, the earth itself moved symbolically. This was the result of the publication of another earth-shattering manuscript, in 1543, *De Revolutionibus Orbium Coelestium* by Copernicus. From now on the earth we live in 'vacated its position at the centre of the universe and took up station as one of several planets circling the sun.'[1] The earth as we knew it in the Middle Ages was dead.

It is no surprise that in a Europe saturated by Christian theology, Christ's death should become the single greatest life-giving force in European art for over a thousand years. Holbein lived 1,500 years after the death of Christ and this fact had its effect on the work of 'the master of realism' as he has been described. Holbein's friend, Oporinus, printed at Basel for Andreas Vesalius a book called *De Humani Corporis Fabrica*, which effected in the world of anatomy what Copernicus introduced to the world of astronomy. Scientific examination replaced metaphysical speculation. Vesalius proposed that the only way to understand the nature and function of human organs was by dissecting cadavers and trusting the evidence of our own fingers touching the tissue, literally by bloodying our hands. Holbein applied such criteria to his own depiction of the human predicament, and especially in his representation of the dead Christ in the tomb.

The first surviving representation of Jesus on the cross is from about 420 and for the next thousand years the passion narrative provided artists with a ready-made series of set-piece scenes. But for all the innumerable crucifixions, depositions and resurrections, there is one episode that has rarely been portrayed: the time between Good Friday and Easter Sunday when Christ was simply dead and his mutilated body was lying in the tomb. This is the subject of one of the most extraordinary images in all religious art, Holbein's *Dead Christ in the Tomb*. He painted it about six years after he arrived in Basel. There can be no doubt that, symbolically, as far as Holbein was concerned, Christ was definitively dead in Basel at this moment in history. His is a painting of unprecedented – and harrowing – realism. Here were the principles of the new anatomy applied to the techniques of artistic representation. Coffin-sized, it shows one panel removed to reveal an emaciated body on a white crumpled shroud. Although *rigor mortis* has set in, the hands and feet still claw in their death agony, the mouth and eyes remain open (see p. 70).

Unconfirmed stories circulated that Holbein painted this elongated corpse from the model of a Jewish man who had died by suicide, drowned in the river Rhine. Holbein's disciples are said to have eventually removed the corpse from his studio because it was decomposing and causing nausea from putrefaction. The picture itself almost corroborates the story. Muscle tone in the body has begun to collapse and the flesh has taken on the green hue of putrefaction (forensic examination has put the degree of corruption as being consistent with a three-day-old corpse.) The man is not handsome, his body is not beautiful: this is painting as *post-mortem*.

We do not know who commissioned the portrait, or why; nor do we know where it was hung. The pierced hand, feet and flank identify the man as Jesus but oddly, for a work of such uncompromising realism, there are no punctures left by the crown of thorns nor marks from the scourging. The first time the painting is mentioned in an inventory it is listed as 'A dead man by Hans Holbein, oil on wood, with the title *Jesus Nazarenus Rex*'. But, even here, the inscription is of a later date and is not by Holbein himself.

Symbolically, as I say, there is no doubt that the artist saw Jesus Christ as dead in Basel in the year 1521. It was not three days, but rather three centuries later before this corpse would rise again artistically.

On his way from Baden to Geneva in August, 1867, Dostoyevsky stopped at Basel, where he viewed Hans Holbein's painting. In her memoirs, Anna Grigorevna recounts leaving her husband alone and returning fifteen to twenty minutes later to find him 'riveted to the spot' before it: 'in his agitated face there was a kind of frightened expression, one which I had happened to notice more than once in the first minutes of an epileptic fit.' Afterwards Dostoyevsky told his wife 'one could lose one's faith from that picture'. Besides this cryptic remark, repeated later by Myshkin in *The Idiot*, Dostoyevsky's only commentary on the painting comes through the voice of Ippolit in that same novel:

The picture represented Christ just taken down from the cross … In the painting his face is dreadfully disfigured by blows, swollen, covered with terrible swollen and bloody bruises, the eyes open, the pupils turned up, the large open whites of the eyes bright with a sort of deathly, glassy reflection … As one looks at that painting, one conceives of nature in the form of some huge, implacable, dumb beast, or to be more exact, to be much more exact, though it may seem strange, in the form of some huge machine of the latest design which, deaf and unfeeling, has senselessly seized, crushed, and swallowed up a great and priceless being, a being worth all of nature and its laws, all the earth, which was perhaps created solely for the advent of that being![2]

With his *Dead Christ*, Holbein paints at the representational limits of Dostoyevsky's realism. Dostoyevsky believed that any portrait of the complete and perfect man must somehow be a portrait of Christ. Many of his novels are an avowed attempt to achieve such a portrait. *The Idiot* comes between *The Possessed* and *The Brothers Karamazov* and it grapples with the problem of Christ's character and career as possibly something harmful and even destructive because of his exorbitant compassion and reckless self-abandon. The first part of the novel was written in the space of twenty-three days between two bouts of epilepsy. Holbein's picture is found hanging in Rogozhin's rooms. The picture is the cataclysmic fuse for the novel.[3]

Such spiritual tradition in the world of art is almost as immediate and direct as sexual transmission. Art is always first to intuit and the traces it leaves behind are scented like spoor by those similarly gifted. Art is original in a way that speaks directly to originality. In the Hebrew Bible epilepsy was regarded as a 'sacred' disease, the disease of the prophets. There is a link, especially in this instance of the viewing of Holbein's painting and the writing of his novel, which connects Dostoyevsky's epilepsy with clairvoyance. Writing in 1945, in his preface to an American edition of Dostoyevsky's novels, Thomas Mann suggests:

> I don't know what neurologists think of the 'sacred' disease, but in my opinion it is definitely rooted in the realm of the sexual, it is a wild and explosive manifestation of sex dynamics, a transferred and transfigured sexual act, a mystic dissipation. I regard the subsequent state of contrition and misery, the mysterious feeling of guilt, as even more revealing than the preceding seconds of bliss for which 'one is ready to exchange his life'. No matter to what extent the malady menaced Dostoyevsky's mental powers, it is certain that his psychological insight, his understanding of crime and of what the Apocalypse calls 'satanic depths' and most of all his ability to suggest secret guilt and to weave it into the background of his frequently horrible creatures – all these are inseparably related to the disease.

In 1525 the factional strife that accompanied the Reformation made Basel a place not only where Christ was dead, in the sense that universal love of any kind was an impossibility, but also a difficult place for an artist to work. Protestantism, which had been introduced there as early as 1522, grew considerably in strength and importance during the ensuing four years. By 1526 severe iconoclastic riots denouncing the sinfulness of art, and accompanied by strict censorship of the press swept over the city. 'The arts here are freezing' Erasmus wrote commending the painter to his friends, among them Sir Thomas More. Holbein, carrying this letter of introduction, arrived in London. He met with a favorable reception and stayed there for two years. One of his first jobs in England was to prepare a large portrait of that other great scholar's family, and some detailed studies for this work are still preserved at Windsor Castle. In 1528 he returned to Basel, where he painted portraits and murals for the town hall. In 1532 he left his wife and children in Switzerland and traveled once again to London. If he hoped to get away from the turmoil of the Reformation he must have been disappointed by later events, but when he finally settled in England and was given the official title of court painter by Henry VIII, he found a sphere of activity which allowed him to live and work. He could no longer paint Madonnas, but the tasks of a court painter were varied and absorbing. He designed jewelry and furniture, costumes for pageantries and decorations for halls, weapons and goblets. His main job, however, was to paint portraits of the royal household, and it is thanks to Holbein's unfailing eye that we have such a vivid picture of the men and women of Henry VIII's court.[4]

The more than one hundred miniature and full-size portraits he completed provide a remarkable document of that colourful period. An old account of his services relates that he painted the portrait of the king 'life size, so well that everyone who looks [at it] is astonished, since it seems to live as if it moved its head and limbs'. In 1539, when Henry was thinking of marrying Anne of Cleves, he sent Holbein to paint her portrait. So delighted with the portrait was Henry that he raced to the quay side where she was landing to get a first sighting of his bride to be. When he saw what she actually looked like, the story goes, Henry was so angry with Holbein, believing that he had deliberately duped him with a false portrait, that he fired him on the spot. The story is hardly true, historians tell us. What is true is that Anne did not look as well as the portrait suggested and Henry infamously referred to her as the 'Flanders mare.' Jonathan Jones suggests:

> So many of the people in Holbein's portraits were killed
> by Henry VIII, there's something eerie about walking

'My Father's Son'

Josephine and John

'Mother's Boy'

John Harlin from Sunday Telegraph

Triangular Tree

Circular Tree

*Arched Bridge between
Sequoia and Oak*

Gate to Graveyard

Glenstal Abbey

le Chateau d'If

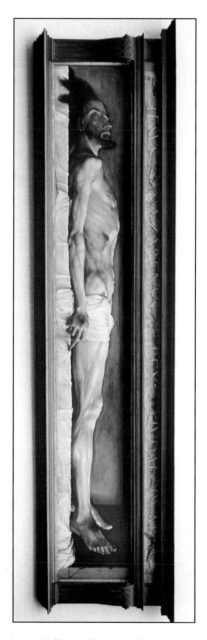

Holbein: The Dead Christ

Holbein: Derich Born

Holbein: The Ambassadors

among the victims of the most cataclysmic change in British history – the Reformation that Henry initiated in his desperation for a divorce. It killed Thomas More. It nearly killed Thomas Wyatt, who was imprisoned in the Tower as a suspected lover of Anne Boleyn and saw her execution from his window. At the centre of this carnival of death stood the monumental, increasingly corpulent king. In the Tower of London you can see his massive suit of armour with trimmings by Holbein. At Tate Britain, he looms over you and his pig-like head, its neck a thick trunk, slides into a gold-laced collar in the oppressively ornate painting lent from the Thyssen.[5]

In 1543, Holbein, in London working on another portrait of the king, died, a victim of the plague. Ten years earlier he had painted a very splendid portrait of a young German working in London called Derich Born (see p. 71). This portrait is like a symbol of the shifting world and the changing times: the whole country of England emerging from the Middle Ages and displaying itself in the 'studied Renaissance nonchalance' recently perfected by Italian artists. This is, says Waldemar Januszczak, art critic for *The Sunday Times*, 'someone 500 years ago already imagining he is James Dean'. But it is Holbein who makes him so, it is Holbein who transforms England from a medieval backwater into a Renaissance state. This 'pasty-faced youth in a big man's pose' is Holbein's creation. The inscription under the parapet on which Derich is Born reveals Holbein himself recognising this truth: 'Add but the voice and you have his whole self, that you may doubt whether the painter or the father has made him.' This person is more a creation of Holbein's than he is of his own father. 'This isn't just an important moment in British history … this is the übermoment, the one that propels and defines everything that follows. To have an artist as great as Holbein on hand to supply such tactile evidence of these years is a tremendous piece of luck.' But is it simply luck? Holbein came to England first to work for the benighted Thomas More and so arrived at the beginning of the series of extraordinary events which led to the 'volcanic split with the Roman Catholic Church'. What was Holbein's view about all this? Can we tell from closer examination of his work?

Holbein's Secret

Holbein's portrait of the ambassadors Jean de Dinteville (1504–1555) and Georges de Selve (1509–1541) in the National Gallery in London is an example of the kind of internal cryptic or secret symbolism which could be used in artistic works to convey messages to those in the know, but which remain opaque to those who can no longer interpret. It is a symbolism designed to occlude.

Painted on ten oak panels joined vertically, the so-called portrait presents two men on either side of a double-decker table facing the viewer. The background is a green, almost theatrical, damask curtain; the floor a reproduction of the pavement in the sanctuary of Westminster Abbey. At an angle across the pavement, in the middle foreground, is an elongated anamorphosis of a human skull. Half concealed behind the green curtain on the top left-hand side is a tiny silver crucifix. Occupying the centre of the panel are a number of identifiable objects which, from their central position and painstaking rendition, seem to upstage the two ambassadors. On the lower shelf of the table are a globe of the world, an eleven-stringed lute with one conspicuously broken string, an open hymn book, an arithmetic text, which is closed but marked with a set-square, a pair of dividers and a case of flutes; on the top shelf of the same table: an astronomical globe, a cylindrical dial, two quadrants, a torquetum, a polyhedral sundial, a closed book, and one smaller dial, all placed on a highly ornate turkey rug, draped as a table-cloth over the top half of the table.[1] All of these objects have a meaning and a position other and more than their almost perfect representation of themselves as still life objects in an observable world. They form a jigsaw of meaning quite hidden from the casual observer. They are alive with symbolic discharge and phosphoresence. One would need to be almost an artistic detective to uncover the symbolic meaning of this painting almost five hundred years after this suggestive deed was done.

The contrast between the two men on either side of the table is striking. A black ermine-lined coat over a slashed rose-red satin doublet gives Dinteville the impressive physique of a French diplomat. He wears a jauntily angled black cap and carries in his right hand a dagger in a golden sheath. The hilt of his sword is visible at his waist. Intelligent, humorous, exuding panache, this man gets things done: a mover and a shaker. De Selve, the bishop, wearing 'a long gown of murrey-coloured brocade lined with sable' which he clutches around him is, history relates, of saintly character and outstanding ability.[2] He seems to shrink back and defer to the other. On the table between them are the instruments which science and culture, art and astronomy have provided as tools with which to fashion the world at their disposal. They are prototypes of the ambassadors negotiating a new world. Between them they have the competence, the sensitivity and the skill necessary to make the future happen in an imaginative way. Scarlet and black, they represent the two major forces of politics and religion which defined the Middle Ages, ushered in the Renaissance and now stand in readiness as the future approaches.

But what is that ugly elongated fishlike skull in so central a position? For many years people did not recognise it for what it was. If you stand in the National Gallery in London with your ear to the wall on the right-hand side of the painting and look at it laterally, the skull assumes its correct proportions and the viewer is stunned by the accuracy of the representation and the cleverness of the artist's achievement in so startling an effect. This is certainly, in some way or other, Holbein's signature in a central place. It is more than simply a conventional memento mori; some suggest that the words *hohles Gebein*, meaning 'hollow bone', combine to make up Hol-bein's name. However, there is surely more to it than that. You realise that you have been forced into this awkward position, against the wall beside the painting, for a purpose. It is from this angle that the whole picture should be viewed. Looking up from the skull your eye catches the eye on the face of the body hanging from the half-hidden silver cross. Such a line from the eye of the observer, with right ear to the wall, to the dying head of Christ, passes through the brightest star in the most prominent constellation on the celestial globe, placed on the uppermost shelf of the table between the two men. The star is Deneb and the constellation is Cygnus. Symbolic of France perhaps, its stars form a very pronounced 'Latin' cross (perhaps the one seen in the vision of the Emperor Constantine) but, more crucially in this context, contained within the figure of a bird flying downwards vertically. So, the artist has forced us to take our rightful place and to assume the correct posture for viewing his picture. The details arranged within the painting reveal themselves to be coded alphabets which allow us to decipher the secret which the ambassadors seek to convey about a mystery of a certain moment in time.

The day is Good Friday, 11 April 1533. (If thirty-three was the age of Christ at his death, this date marks fifteen centuries, a millennium and a half, since his crucifixion.) The skull casts its shadow at an unnatural angle, but this angle correctly represents the time recorded in various ways in the painting, for that Good Friday. The religious meaning of *The Ambassadors* (see p. 72) is suggested by the recurrence of the theme involving the number twenty-seven. This number is a factor found three times on the open page of the arithmetic book. As a pure number twenty-seven is thrice thrice three, and three is the number of the Trinity (twelfth-century Neoplatonist William of Conches took the numerical relationship of the Platonic twenty-seven and the number of the Trinity as an argument for the very identity of the Holy Spirit). With the Reformation, and new emphasis on the personal experience of believers, the Holy Spirit gained rather than lost importance. The Latin hymn writers had helped to stabilise theological language and imagery most conclusively with the hymn '*Veni Creator Spiritus*' and its later partner '*Veni Sancte Spiritus*'. The open hymnal on the lower shelf of the stand in the picture is Luther's version of '*Veni Sancte Spiritus*'. In his first preface to this hymnal, Luther would 'see all the arts, and music in particular, used in the service of him who hath given and created them' as opposed to the narrow and widespread prejudice 'that all sciences should be battered and annihilated by the Gospel, as some fanatics would have them'.

John North, from whose book *The Ambassadors' Secret*[3] I take much of the analysis above, sees between the two figures in the picture an invisible hexagram (star) with wide bands or borders encompassing the two triangles of which it is shaped. He draws confidence for this suggestion from the already included hexagon ('Solomon's seal' or 'Star of David') half hidden in the innermost circle of the pavement floor. 'If we choose the same proportional value for it in the upper hexagram as we find in the pavement, then several unforeseen properties of the scheme emerge immediately:

- The edge of the table runs along the inside of one component triangle, and the polyhedral dial fits snugly into one angle of it.

- The first white line of the turkey rug below the table edge defines the outside of that same triangle.

- The vertical diameter of the circle (the plumbline of the compound instrument) passes through the middle of the horizontal 'S' motif on the turkey rug.'

Whatever about the details of this description, the picture then becomes a 'reading' of events on this day in England where and when the artist was painting. The angle from which we view both the painting and the world is all-important. The artist seems to be forcing us to stand with our ear pressed to the wall listening for as yet unheard music, and our eyes fixed on the half-hidden crucifix as focal point for identifying the rest. One cannot be precise about the time of the act of painting the picture, John North tells us, but everything in the picture points towards a particular date as its exact point of reference: 11 April 1533.

By this date Cranmer had been made Archbishop of Canterbury, Anne Boleyn was pregnant with Elizabeth I of England, Catherine of Aragon had been told that she was no longer Queen of England. Cranmer had asked Henry VIII that he be allowed 'to determine his great cause of matrimony'. Why else had he been consecrated archbishop? The break with Rome was inevitable. Pope Clement declared Cranmer's judgement null and void. No wonder the string on the eleven-stringed lute, symbol of harmony and peace, is broken. And yet the message of this painting could be that the Holy Spirit is the invisible star at the centre of every particular situation and, as such, encompasses all the scientific, artistic and religious striving of the world in which we live. All three persons of the Trinity are at work to use this particular Good Friday situation to the best advantage of the emerging future of humanity.

The position and point of view we adopt influences the way we view everything that happens, and the presence of an unseen geometry at the centre of any picture alters any eventual interpretation or perspective. Everything in Christian history is measured from the time and location of Christ's intervention, so that our deliberations occur with reference to the place of the skull, Golgotha. Thus the symbolic presence of the hideous and enigmatic anamorphosis of the human skull in the middle foreground. But such measurement is conducted with the instruments available to us, most important of which is the unseen agency of the third Person of the Trinity who makes real for us the presence of whatever time we choose to commemorate. *Anamnesis* without *epiclesis* is a blank. Without the particular kind of remembering (*Anamnesis* in Greek) of salvation history, that everything that happens is a symbol of our rescue operation, and without the specific invocation (*Epiclesis* in Greek) of the power of the Holy Spirit, history of whatever date remains irrevocably concealed behind impenetrable damask curtains. The lemniscate 'S' at the centre of the rug, at the centre of the picture, brands the space and time of this portrait with the seal of the Spirit, making its geography universal, its history actual. We are present at the moment it was painted. Such creativity provides the magic carpet which carries us to where the inspiration took place. It is original. It conceals the x-ray of its origin, the finger of the Spirit. Such is one way of reading the history of artistic expression symbolically.

Vincent van Gogh

Three hundred and fifty years later, almost contemporary to Dostoyevsky, Vincent van Gogh provides the second example of artistic symbolism. The standard version of his life and work suggests that he was a fanatical Christian for the first twenty-five years of his life. He then threw that religiosity aside at the age of twenty-seven and became an artist. This was fortunate for the world of art because he produced an extraordinary number of great paintings during the next ten years of his artistic life before he took his own life at the age of thirty-seven in 1890.

As this second example, van Gogh can be used to explain the sense and symbolism of liturgy through both his life and his work. He was fanatically Christian at the beginning of his life it is true. He later abandoned this version of religion and turned to painting, this is also true. However, to describe this as a turn from religion to atheism and a liberating movement which allowed the artist to emerge from the ashes of the Christian is false.

Examination of his correspondence will confirm that it was a new way of finding expression for his passionate belief in God and in Christianity, one which joined his own century and its preoccupations to the more ancient traditions, while it did indeed discard the narrow and hypocritical theology of his Dutch family and their forbears. In other words, van Gogh's art, like liturgy, was a way of expressing the mystery of his life with

God in a new language. 'Do this in memory of me' is precisely what Vincent did in his extraordinary artwork.

So, in much the same way that our only reliable access to the mystery of the life, death and resurrection of Jesus Christ is through the liturgical celebration of 'his' mysteries, so too, the only real access we have to the religious being of Vincent van Gogh is through the artworks which he left behind for us. In examining these and retrieving the mystery which they unfold, we have a template and a workshop which can help us to understand the ways in which we should examine the liturgy to detect how it too reveals for us the mysteries of Jesus Christ. There is a similar distance, and a corresponding switch of idiom, between the life and person of Jesus Christ and the liturgy which we celebrate to make us aware of his presence, as there is between Vincent van Gogh and the works which he left behind him.

We have to begin with some history. Vincent's father and his uncle were both clergyman, theologians and preachers. They were Dutch Reformed Protestants but not Calvinists as many have suggested. They were, to be precise, Groningens, named after the theological faculty of that school. These, like the modernists, were affected by the turmoil of the nineteenth century and were more open to such innovations as biblical criticism. They were opposed to the more radical Calvanist notions of predestination or the total depravity of humankind. The biggest influence on them was probably Friedrich Schleiermacher (1768–1834), the German theologian and philosopher, who was on terms of intimate friendship with the Romanticists, especially Schlegel. He sympathised with many of their aims, yet with a conviction of the necessity of religion which they did not share. So, whereas Vincent's family was not as open and as enlightened as he might have hoped, they were not as closed and narrow-minded as some biographers have suggested. One of Vincent's favourite quotations was from

Victor Hugo: '*Les religions passent mais Dieu demeure.*'[1] In his reminiscences P.C. Gorlitz tells us:

> When Sunday came, van Gogh would go to church three times, either to the Roman Catholic Church, or to the Protestant or Old Episcopal Church, which was commonly called the Jansenist Church. When once we made the remark, 'How is it possible to go to three different churches of such divergent creeds?' he said: 'Well, in every church I see God, and it's all the same to me whether a Protestant pastor or a Roman Catholic priest preaches; it is not really a matter of dogma, but of the spirit of the Gospel, and I find this spirit in all churches.'[2]

It was a Franciscan type of piety that inspired Vincent, as indeed it had inspired the Dutch mystic, Gerhard Groote, who founded the Brethren of the Common Life, and which produced, in turn, Thomas à Kempis and *The Imitation of Christ*. It was also this type of piety that inspired John Bunyan as he wrote *The Pilgrim's Progress* from his prison cell.[3] These were the books that most influenced Vincent.

He studied theology with his uncle, Joannes Paulus Stricker, who was quite a famous theological teacher and preacher, and who wrote several books about his own synthesis of the Christian message. This uncle had a daughter, Kee, whose one-year-old baby son died just as Vincent came to live in Amsterdam, leaving her one surviving child, seven-year-old Joannes Paulus, named after her father. Her husband Dr Christoffel Martinus Vos had taken ill with a 'lung disease' that forced him to abandon his teaching post. Vincent saw in Kee and Vos the ideal of hearth and home. On 27 October 1878, Vos died. Vincent was in love with Kee. He wrote to Theo, his brother: 'To express my feelings for Kee, I said "She, and no other". And her "no, never, never" was not strong enough to make me give her up.' Kee's parents refused to let Vincent near their daughter. 'Your persistence is disgusting,' they told him. 'I put my hand in the flame of the lamp and said, "Let me see her for as long as I can keep my hand in the flame." But they blew out the lamp.' This obsession and his fanatical attempts to adopt a life of total poverty and self-denial caused his father and his uncle huge concern. Even at this early stage they considered committing him to an asylum. Vincent saw them both as hypocrites. He was simply living out the very reality which they had so carefully taught him, and which they now condemned in him as madness. However, Vincent continued to love and admire his father. He wrote to Theo (10 February 1878):

> As you know, Father has been here, and I am so glad he came. You can imagine how the days flew by.
>
> After I had seen Father off at the station and had watched the train go out of sight, even the smoke of it, I came home to my room and saw Father's chair standing near the little table on which the books and copy books of the days before were still lying; and though I know we shall see each other again soon, I cried like a child.

Vincent could not do the kind of study which would have allowed him to follow in the footsteps of his father and his uncle, so he determined to become a simple preacher of the gospel and live in poverty with the poorest of the poor. He selected as his sample of such unfortunates the mostly Catholic miners in Belgium and began to fulfil his evangelical calling by setting out on his own to the coal mining district of the Belgian Borinage to preach the gospel.

Impressed by his commitment, the *Comité de la Société Evangélique Belge* decided to support him on a six-month basis, beginning in January, 1879, in the village of Wasmes. In July they decided not to renew his trial position. He lacked the capacity to preach effectively. His father came to collect him and to bring him home to a more measured life. Van Gogh eventually quarrelled with him, left the house and abandoned the religion of his family. He began his life as an artist.

In 1880 Vincent left behind the evangelical views he espoused as a missionary and focused instead on his life as an artist, on the struggle to reconcile the traditions of the past with the concerns of contemporaneity. He expressed both his filial piety and his new commitment in his *Still Life with Bible and Zola's Joie de Vivre* which he painted in the months following his father's death. The juxtaposition of his father's open Bible with this quintessential modern novel was the symbol of his new synthesis. It also announced his aim to parallel Zola's achievement in painting. 'This one thing remains,' he writes to Theo (early February 1886), 'faith; one feels instinctively that an enormous number of things are changing and that everything will change. We are living in the last quarter of a century that will end again in a tremendous revolution.' And again to Theo (19 November 1881): 'Have no doubt of God's help if you do what God wants you to do, and God wants us in these days to reform the world by renewing the light and the fire of eternal love.' He saw Jesus as 'the supreme artist, more of an artist than all others, disdaining marble and clay and colour, working in the living flesh' (23 June 1888).

He found almost as much prejudice and conservatism in the artistic world which was now his milieu as he had in the religious world of his earlier endeavours: 'I must tell you that with evangelists it is the same as with artists. There is an old academic school, often detestable, tyrannical, the accumulation of horrors, men who wear a cuirass, a steel armour of prejudices and conventions.'[4]

In 1881 he took in his care a pregnant prostitute whom he called Sien and employed her as a model. Her daughter Maria and she became his holy family and he decided to marry Sien.

His heroic gesture was ironically spurned by Sien's mother, herself with eleven illegitimate children, who decided that Vincent was not a suitable match for her daughter.

One of the indications that his newly adopted avocation was in direct line with his earlier one is the fact that he painted more than thirty representations of sowers who went out to sow the seed, and that *The Raising of Lazarus, The Good Samaritain* and *The Pietà,* which were copies of earlier religious masterpieces, depict Christ with the features of his own face.

Vincent's symbolic art became the expression of the infinite in the mundane and the numinous in day-to-day existence. This was his vision of resurrected life, 'an existence changed by a phenomenon no more surprising than the transformation of the caterpillar into a butterfly, or of the white grub into a cockchafer' (23 June 1888).

'Il s'agit de saisir ce qui ne passe pas dans ce qui passe'[5] he quotes Gavarni. This is not pantheism as some have suggested but, perhaps, more accurately a theology of panentheism where God is seen in and through nature – nature being, in this sense, symbolic: 'all Nature seems to speak; and going home, one has the same feeling as when one has finished a book by Victor Hugo, for instance. As for me, I cannot understand why everybody does not see it and feel it; Nature or God does it for everyone who has eyes and ears and a heart to understand. For this reason I think a painter is happy because he is in harmony with Nature as soon as he can express a little of what he sees' (to Theo, 27 November 1882). Nature as symbol or sacrament is mediator of the mystical journey to attain knowledge of the divine. 'Aspirations toward the Infinite of which the sower, the sheaf are the symbols still enchant me' he writes in a letter of 18 June 1888. *The Potato Eaters* is his version of the Eucharist – the only 'sacrament' we can be sure was instituted by Christ himself. In this painting, the colour yellow and the symbol of light, the burning lamp, are artistic devices to convey the presence of the

divine. The potato being the food of the ordinary people in their homes is the Eucharistic element.

The colour yellow for Vincent symbolises divine presence which explains his attachment to the *Tournesol* (sunflower) (see p. 105) as well as to the sun. Yellow features prominently in his depictions of sowing and harvesting. In his painting, *The Sower*, van Gogh explains his intention of representing the presence of Christ through the symbolic use of colour, particularly a golden citron-yellow: 'This is the point ... a little citron-yellow for the nimbus [in Delacroix *The Christ in the Boat*] the halo speaks a symbolic language through colour alone' (28 June 1888). 'If I stay here [Saint-Rémy] I shall not try to paint *Christ in the Garden of Olives*, but the glowing of the olives as you still see it, giving nevertheless the exact proportions of the human figure in it, perhaps that would make people think' (L614, 17 November, Letters 3:229). 'Morning light portends Christ's resurrection, with a sun flooding everything with a light of pure gold' (6 September 1889). 'I want to paint men and women with something of the eternal which the halo used to symbolize, and which we seek to convey by the actual radiance and vibration of our colouring' (3 September 1888).

These artistic works of Vincent van Gogh remain behind like sacraments (time/space capsules of a different dimension) revealing to those who have eyes to see this new sense and symbolism with which he incarnated the mystery of the presence of God in our world. His paintings are liturgies which unfold the mystery of God's presence in our day-to-day world, more powerfully, perhaps, than any written word can do. Learning to be in the presence of such artworks is akin to learning how liturgy can move us towards life.

But van Gogh was even more ambitious. He wanted to start a revolution, a new movement in painting which would revive the religious symbolism of humankind. Religion and art would meet together in the Yellow House which he established in Arles for this elevated purpose. He selected Paul Gaugin as his partner in the inauguration of this movement and invited the older painter to join him in his ambitious plans. He and Gaugin lived and worked together in Arles, in southern France, for nine weeks in 1888. Van Gogh had rented a small house on a public square, painted yellow, the symbolic colour, which he envisioned as the embodiment of the art of the future. Those who might join him would be the 'Apostles of art'. In preparing for the arrival of the first 'Apostle,' he bought twelve chairs to decorate the house. In mid-September van Gogh himself moved into the Yellow House. His idea of the roles that he and Gaugin would play emerged in the self-portraits that they exchanged early in October. Van Gogh appears in the guise of a bonze, or Buddhist monk, looking past and beyond the viewer with purposeful gaze. Gaugin portrayed himself as Jean Valjean, the character in Victor Hugo's *Les Misèrables.* Van Gogh was taken aback when he received the portrait: he saw a desperation and a pessimism; not what he expected from the designated head of the Studio of the South.

The two artists talked about the modern artist taking the role of a prophet, following in the footsteps of Christ. Gaugin had painted *Vision of the Sermon* in an innovative attempt to depict religious experience in a modern style. By December, however, the artists' differences were erupting into stormy debates. The more van Gogh worried about Gaugin's leaving, the more Gaugin prepared to do so. The partnership ended explosively on 23 December and Gaugin left Arles the next day. This was the famous episode after which van Gogh cut off his ear and presented it to a prostitute in his favourite brothel at Arles.

All we have now left of the Yellow House are the paintings of it which Van Gogh did at this time (see p. 106). The house itself was destroyed during the war. Nothing of it now remains.

The *Starry Night,* which Vincent painted in June 1889, is an autobiographical landscape which can be divided into three separate areas: the village scene, the cypress tree, the sky (see p. 107). The church provides a focal point and a vertical accent in the village scene. While every house glows with yellow light under the brilliance of the starry sky, the church remains completely dark. It demonstrates Vincent's journey from the darkness inside the church to the triumph of the mystic's communion with God through nature. The cypress shoots into the firmament like a giant flame as the ultimate union of the soul with the infinite. But it is the sky full of radiant light and pulsating rhythms, symbolic of infinity, that dominates. This great coiling spiral nebula with eleven stars and an orange moon is resurrection. 'God is a lighthouse in eclipse,' Vincent quotes Victor Hugo.[6]

In a portrait of Eugene Boch, van Gogh explains his symbolic use of deep blue to evoke the notion of infinity: 'Behind the head, instead of painting the ordinary wall of the mean room, I paint infinity, a plain background of the richest, intensest blue that I can contrive' (11 August 1888).

In a letter to Theo (3 February 1889), the year before his death, he writes: 'But as for considering myself as completely sane, we must not do it. People here who have been ill like me have told me the truth. You may be old or young, but there will always be moments when you lose your head.' Van Gogh was perceived to be mad and was locked up in an asylum at the request of his neighbours. He himself knew that what they called 'madness' was really his own attempt to reach the truth about himself in the deepest recesses of his being, which was also the truth about his neighbours. He had written to Theo some years earlier (October 1883):

> They said I was out of my mind, but I knew myself that it was not true, for the very reason that I felt my own disease deep within me, and tried to remedy it. I exhausted myself in hopeless unsuccessful efforts, it is true, but

> because of that fixed idea of reaching a normal point of
> view again, I never mistook my own desperate doings,
> worryings and drudgings for my real innermost self.

Van Gogh left behind at least forty-three portraits of himself as
testament to the fact that he was not 'mad,' and as introductions
to himself as he really was (see p. 108). Self-portraiture was the
struggle to 'remain human' in a society hostile both to himself
and to the arts. 'I should like to paint portraits,' he writes in
1890, 'which would appear after a century to the people living
then as apparitions.' We are the people living a hundred years
later.

His wonderfully moving face bears witness to the loneliness
and sense of failure of a misunderstood genius. How many
people today does he represent? A year before he shot himself in
despair and died he wrote to Theo (19 June 1889):
'Unfortunately we suffer from the circumstances and the ills of
the times in which we live, for better or for worse.' In September
of that same year before he died, he again wrote to his brother: 'I
with my mental disease, I keep thinking of so many other artists
suffering mentally, and I tell myself that this does not prevent
one from exercising the painter's profession as if nothing were
amiss.' Vincent left his self-portraits to a future generation who
might understand him better. He saw himself as 'a link in the
chain of artists', a pathfinder for future generations. He was a
selfless worker towards a new society which would be energised
and nourished by the arts. 'There is an art of the future,' he says
of a self-portrait dedicated to Gaugin, 'and it is going to be so
lovely and so young that, even if we give up our youth for it, we
must gain in serenity.'

And which of us can look, without some sense of guilt about
so-called sanity, at the last self-portrait in unbuttoned coat
against a background of rhythmically whirling spirals, painted in
Saint-Rémy some months before he died, now hanging in the

Museum of Modern Art, New York. Here is the last look of an artist before he goes into the darkness against which he struggled as a painter for thirty-seven years. He never sold a single painting during his life time, except one to his brother, Theo. He had to beg for the money to buy the yellow ochre that he used to paint the picture which a hundred years later was sold in Sotheby's for over £6 million. Is it not ironical that as I write these lines in May 2006 a portrait which Vincent painted in 1890 of l'Arlesienne, Madame Ginoux, who owned the café near the Yellow House and whose signature is on the document asking for his removal to an asylum,[7] sold for $40 million at an auction in Christies of London. Theo had written to his own wife in 1888 about his brother: 'If it had been granted to him once to find someone to whom he could pour out his heart, it might never have come to this.'

There are two aspects to our lives here on earth. There is the horizontal, biological, natural life from birth to death: 'We are born, we work, we love, we grow, we vanish' (L76, 9 October 1876) as Vincent describes it. But there is another dimension which is the vertical one of resurrection. At each moment of our natural lives we can perform some action which transforms what we are doing into an eternal and enduring reality. This is achieved through the power of love. It is a sacrament whereby the ordinary everyday humdrum existence of each one of us can be transubstantiated into divine life, into eternal life. This means that the vertical power of resurrected life is everywhere present in our universe and any element, or thing, or person, in our world can be the bread and wine which is transformed into this body and blood. Vincent was able to see this dimension of reality everywhere in the world around him. His paintings of the natural world are imbued with this energy. This is what gives his pictures their hypnotic power and makes them compelling whether or not we are aware of what we see. 'That brings up again the eternal question: Is the whole of life visible to us, or isn't it rather that this side of death we see only one hemisphere?' Vincent describes how each one of us acts as if the earth is flat and horizontal, even though it has been proved to us by science that it is round. 'Just like our ancestors before the discovery of the roundness, we continue to use the earth, for all practical purposes, as if it were flat. Now this is true also about life and death. Death is the other side of the world we live in. It leads us into the other hemisphere.' Just as we take the train to get to Tarasçon or Rouen, we take death to reach a star. Vincent himself took death to reach that star when he shot himself in the chest and died two days later on 29 July 1890. That was how he reached the star he had painted so often, because, as he said to his brother: '…To die quietly of old age would be to go there on foot' (9 July 1888).

A Pair
of Worn Shoes

In his essay entitled 'The Origin of the Work of Art' Martin Heidegger interprets a painting of a pair of shoes by van Gogh (see p. 109) in order to suggest that art can disclose truth. The painting to which Heidegger refers is simply a pair of rather worn shoes, facing forward, with the laces undone. There are no other discernible objects or items. Heidegger, one of the most gifted metaphysicians and philosophers of the twentieth century, believes that he can, with reference to the painting alone, penetrate to its essence:

> There is nothing surrounding this pair of peasant shoes in or to which they might belong, only an undefined space. There are not even clods from the soil of the field or the path through it sticking to them, which might at least hint at their employment. A pair of peasant shoes and nothing more. And yet.

And yet, Heidegger will examine this artwork in itself, and explain its deeper meaning:

> From the dark opening of the worn insides of the shoes the toilsome tread of the worker stands forth. In the stiffly solid heaviness of the shoes there is the accumulated tenacity of her slow trudge through the far-spreading and

ever-uniform furrows of the field, swept by a raw wind. On the leather there lies the dampness and saturation of the soil. Under the soles there slides the loneliness of the field-path as the evening declines. In the shoes there vibrates the silent call of the earth, its quiet gift of the ripening corn and its enigmatic self-refusal in the fallow desolation of the wintry field. This equipment is pervaded by uncomplaining anxiety about the certainty of bread, the wordless joy of having once more withstood want, the trembling before the advent of birth and shivering at the surrounding menace of death. This equipment belongs to the earth and it is protected in the world of the peasant woman. From out of this protected belonging the equipment itself rises to its resting-in-self.

This is a beautifully expressed interpretation, which examines this artwork as a thing in itself and makes no reference to its symbolic possibilities or its numinous inspiration in the life of the artist. It is an example of how one of the most intelligent thinkers the world has known can fail to understand the double meaning of a particular fragment of creation, because he refuses to entertain any reality other than the obverse appearance of things in the world around us.

Going from what might be considered a minimalist interpretation of the shoes to a more extravagant one, Meyer Shapiro (1904–1996), the world-renowned art historian, disputes Heidegger's attribution of van Gogh's shoes to a peasant woman, insisting that the shoes in the painting belong to van Gogh himself. Restituting the shoes to the signatory of the painting, his essay in interpretation dedicates itself to, as Derrida puts it, 'the immense tide of deportees searching for their names', victims of the violent upheavals of techno-industrial modernity culminating in mass warfare; and indeed to the 'army of ghosts demanding their shoes', those chillingly anonymous shoes piled up at Auschwitz.[1]

Brilliant and persuasive as these two interpretations certainly are they remain heady, intellectual explanations, and, as such, 'the desire for attribution is a desire for appropriation'.[2] Headwork rather than heartwork, to use Rilke's phrase, they both attempt to colonise and recapture the polyvalence and the immensity of the artwork within the domesticated domain of comprehensibility. That Heidegger assigns the shoes to a peasant and Shapiro to the city-dwelling artist is in either case 'properly due' neither to peasant nor painter but to these 'illustrious Western professors' themselves, Derrida continues wryly, so that the attribution says more about them than it does about either the painting or the shoes.

Symbols are their own intractable reality, uncontrollable in terms of epistemology's bridle and bit. And yet they are there to show us a vastness and a possibility way beyond the compass of our mental capacities. They constitute a language, they present a structure, they offer an understanding which we must renounce our limited mindset to engage. If we are to enter the world to which they offer access we have to strip ourselves of the armour, the equipment, the paraphernalia of conquering explorers and sit down patiently to watch, to wait, to attend, to listen.

Paul Gaugin offers another interpretation which opens wider possibilities. He noticed that Vincent kept a pair of badly worn shoes which seemed to have importance for him:

> In the studio was a pair of big hob-nailed shoes, all worn and spotted with mud; he made of it a remarkable still life painting. I do not know why I sensed that there was a story behind this old relic, and I ventured one day to ask him if he had some reason for preserving with respect what one ordinarily throws out for the rag-picker's basket.

And so Vincent begins to recount the tale of these worn-out shoes.

My father was a pastor, and at his urging I pursued theological studies in order to prepare for my future vocation. As a young pastor I left for Belgium one fine morning, without telling my family, to preach the gospel in the factories, not as I had been taught but as I understood it myself. These shoes, as you see, have bravely endured the fatigue of that trip.

It turns out, Gaugin continues, that 'preaching to the miners in the Borinage, Vincent undertook to nurse a victim of the fire in the mine. The man was so badly burned and mutilated that the doctor had no hope for his recovery. Only a miracle, he thought, could save him. Van Gogh tended him forty days with loving care and saved the miner's life.' Gaugin then tells of the explosion in the mine:

Chrome yellow overflowed, a terrible fiery glow … The creatures who crawled at that moment … said 'adieu' to life that day, goodbye to their fellow-men … One of them horribly mutilated, his face burnt, was picked up by Vincent. 'However,' said the company doctor, 'the man is done for, unless by a miracle …'

Gaugin continues:

Vincent believed in miracles, in maternal care. The madman (decidedly he was mad) sat up, keeping watch forty days, at the dying man's bedside. Stubbornly he kept the air from getting into his wounds and paid for the medicines. A comforting priest (decidedly, he was mad). The patient talked. The mad effort brought a dead Christian back to life … In my yellow room – a small still life: violet that one. Two enormous worn out misshapen shoes. They were Vincent's shoes. Those that he took one fine morning, when they were new, for his journey on foot from Holland to Belgium. The young preacher had just finished his theological studies in order to be a minister like his father. He had gone off to the mines to those whom he called his brothers ... Contrary to the teaching of his wise Dutch professors, Vincent had believed in a Jesus who loved the poor; and his soul, deeply pervaded by charity, sought the consoling words and sacrifice for the weak, and to combat the rich. Very decidedly, Vincent was already mad.

And then a vision came to Vincent which he disclosed to Gaugin, and which explains why these shoes became so important to him. The scars on the man's face – this man resurrected by a miracle of care – looked to Vincent exactly like the scars from a crown of thorns. 'I had,' Vincent says, 'in the presence of this man who bore on his brow a series of scars, a vision of the crown of thorns, a vision of the resurrected Christ.' At this point in telling Gaugin the story, Vincent picks up his brush and says, referring to the 'resurrected Christ': 'And I, Vincent, I painted him.'

Gaugin again takes up the story: 'When we were together in Arles, both of us mad, in continual struggle for beautiful colours, I adored red; where could one find a perfect vermilion? He, with his yellowish brush, traced on the wall which suddenly became violet: "I am whole in Spirit. I am the Holy Spirit."' Gaugin finishes his account: 'And Vincent took up his palette again; silently he worked. Beside him was a white canvas. I began his portrait. I too had the vision of a Jesus preaching kindness and humility.'

'Vincent was already mad' – Gaugin repeats this several times, thick with irony; that we all should be graced enough to touch such madness![3] Ken Wilber continues his own interpretation of the shoes:

… Whatever other interpretations we wish to give to Vincent's vision, the overall evidence most clearly suggests that it was very probably a true vision of the radical potential in all of us. These higher states and visions are sometimes intermixed with personal pathologies or neuroses, but the states themselves are not pathological in their essence; quite the contrary, researchers consistently refer to them as extraordinary states of well-being. Thus, Vincent's central vision itself most likely was not pathological, not psychotic, not madness at all – which is why Gaugin keeps poking fun at those who would think that way: decidedly, he was mad. Which means, decidedly, he was plugged into a reality that we should all be so fortunate to see.

Thus, when Vincent said he saw the resurrected Christ, that is exactly what he meant, and that is very likely exactly what he saw. And thus he carried with him, as a dusty but dear reminder, the shoes in which this vision occurred.

These are the shoes in which Vincent nursed Jesus, the Jesus in all of us.[4]

However we choose to interpret them, the shoes of van Gogh are symbols whose power and polyvalence far exceed any or all the most elegant and convincing explanations. They serve their purpose here as prime examples of the reality of living symbols which help us to become aware of the even more potent and polyvalent varieties which are liturgical symbols. They can describe those empty tombs which are each one of us when we become 'Holy Spirit' and rise from the dead, whether as Belgian miners, Dutch artists, or ordinary viewers of the painting.[5]

The Icon

The third and, from the point of view of this book, most significant example from the history of art is the icon (see p. 110). In 312 the emperor Constantine gave his official support to Christianity. He had seen a cross in the sky and been promised that under this sign he would conquer. Which he did. Eighteen years later he moved the capital of his empire to Byzantium, a small town on the sea of Marmora which he called Constantinople after himself. In 1930, Kemel Ataturk changed its name to Istanbul.

Byzantium was where Greek and Roman art met Asian influence and produced the essentially Christian Byzantine art, characterised most specifically by the icon. Icons are essentially a Christian art form. The word comes from the Greek for an image, and it echoes the words used in the Bible to describe the creation of man and woman in the image of God.

Early Christian art was also painted as a fresco or built as a mosaic. The first of these were painted on masonry coated with layers of plaster (*al fresco* means 'while the plaster is still fresh or wet'); the second was composed of tiny cubes of coloured stone or glass pressed into the plaster.

Not all Christians venerated the icons. Not all religions permit such use of art as a depiction of God. Judaism, from which Christianity was born, is vehemently opposed to any representation of the Godhead which would be a work of human hands. As dutiful heir to the Jewish tradition, the early Church inherited the belief in a God who is, and must always be, beyond our imagining and our powers of description. This remains a constant bedrock of all Judeo-Christian teaching and is a natural attitude of a religion which was characterised by a tradition, over a thousand years old before ever Jesus Christ appeared, forbidding any images of God, even images formed in the mind, even the use of the name of God. Such prohibitions are enshrined in the decalogue: 'You shall not make yourself a graven image or any likeness whatever ...'[1]

It is easy to understand, therefore, how the history of the icon is intimately bound up with the history of Christianity in the first centuries after Christ's death, as the community of Christians tried to work out the precise meaning of the tradition they had inherited: where it was the same as the Jewish tradition and where it differed.

One of the most important moments in this history of discovery of their authentic profile was the iconoclastic crisis. This has been compared with the later crisis in Christendom occasioned by what has become known as The Reformation in the sixteenth century.

Iconoclasm means in Greek 'the smashing of images'. This movement of reform and purification in the Christian Church began in the first quarter of the eighth century, around 725. In this phase of the movement icons were destroyed as pagan images or idols, incompatible with Christian belief and a scandal to Jews and Moslems. In the second phase of the movement, almost a century later, icons were tolerated for pedagogical purposes, almost as a Bible in pictures or comic strips, to teach the illiterate, but they were considered unsuitable for public worship and required to be removed from churches.

It was the Emperor Leo III who initiated the iconoclastic movement in about 726. He may have had all kinds of political or economic reasons for doing so, but his basic reason was to institute a religious reform which would bring Christianity back to its roots, where worship in spirit and in truth would be the norm.[2] He looked around him and saw huge progress being made by the Moslem version of religion, which was emphatically and violently faithful to the principle of imagelessness. Not even animals could be depicted in their places of worship. He interpreted the earthquake in 726 as an expression of divine displeasure at the state of Christendom. Just as the earth had swallowed up Dathan for idolatrous practices, so the earth was swallowing up Christians who had strayed from the path of monotheistic purity.

Leo saw himself as prefigured in the Old Testament by Hezekiah, who destroyed the bronze serpent over the temple in Jerusalem eight hundred years after it had been put there as an object of worship – it being the one Moses had used to stem the plague of serpents in the desert. Leo, eight hundred years after Christianity was born, would perform a similar symbolic act by destroying the bronze image of Christ which was above the entrance to his palace. Thus he would begin the work of saving Christianity from idolatry which had crept in to despoil the original years of simplicity.

During the attempt to destroy these images which had crept into Christianity by the eighth century, Leo III had a number of remarkable military successes over the, up to then, irresistible advance of Islam, which he took as confirmation from the Almighty of the direction he had initiated. So, Leo's son, in turn, the Emperor Constantine V, decided to copperfasten his father's endeavours by calling a Church Council which would endorse the principles of iconoclasm. There were three hundred and thirty-eight bishops at this council which met in Constantinople from 2 February to 8 August 754. Afterwards, it was suggested that the Emperor put undue pressure on the bishops present, but whether he did or didn't, the council ratified the iconoclastic charter which included a lengthy definition which was then promulgated by the Emperor.

Now, many later historians and believers hold that this was a high moment for Christianity and that if the results of this Council had been upheld we wouldn't have had to go through the later 'reformations' which proved so devastating to the unity of Christianity. However, history is written by the winners and the fact is that iconoclasm was defeated, the above council declared heretical, and icons, images, statues, holy pictures and representations of Christ, the Holy Family and the extended family of saints and angels were not just allowed back into our churches and dwelling places but were declared to be an essential part of our Christian heritage.

This war was not won without a great deal of struggle, time, discord and even bloodshed. It took centre stage as the most important battle in Byzantium for nearly a century. Two Church councils were devoted to it entirely until eventually in 787 the movement of iconoclasm was definitively defeated and icons were restored to their rightful place in the Christian scheme of things. So great a victory was hailed by the Church as a new feastday: the feast of Orthodoxy which to this day is celebrated in the Orthodox Church on the first Sunday of every season of Lent.

And most denominations of Christianity are involved in this declaration, including Roman Catholicism, because it was pronounced by the Seventh Ecumenical Council, held in Nicea from 24 September to 23 October and gained eventual recognition by the five great patriarchates of the time: Alexandria, Antioch, Constantinople, Jerusalem and Rome. It states:

> We retain, without introducing anything new ... the representation of painted images ... because of the belief in the true and non-illusory Incarnation of God the Word, for our benefit. For things which presuppose each other are mutually revelatory.

> Since this is the case, following the royal path and teaching divinely inspired by our Holy Fathers and the Tradition of the Catholic Church – for we know that it is inspired by the Holy Spirit who lives in it – we decide in all correctness and after a thorough examination, that, just as the holy and vivifying cross, similarly the holy and precious icons painted with colours ... should be placed in the holy churches ... on walls, on boards, in houses and on roads, whether these are icons of our Lord and Saviour, Jesus Christ, or our Spotless and Sovereign Lady, the holy Mother of God, or the holy angels and holy and venerable saints ...

The promulgation links the icons to the incarnation. If Jesus Christ actually became man and lived an historical life on earth then it must be possible to depict that life and represent his features in pictorial form. Just as the evangelists were able to write down an account of his life and his person in books which have become the definitive scriptures of Christianity, so, too, it must be possible for visual artists to describe him in paint.[3] The Eighth Ecumenical Council (869–870) goes so far as to say: 'The icon of Our Lord and Saviour Jesus Christ should be venerated with esteem equal to that afforded to the book of the holy gospels.'[4]

It was Constantine V, son of the Emperor Leo III who best expressed the difficulty of icon painting: 'We ask you how is it possible to depict Our Lord Jesus Christ who is only one person of two natures, immaterial and material, through their union without confusion?' In other words, he was posing the dilemma for the defenders of icons that if they said the icon was depicting Christ as man only, they were guilty of Nestorianism, the great heresy which separated the human element from the divine; if they said the icon represented Christ as both God and man, they were guilty of the monophysite heresy which refused to separate the incomprehensible divinity from the humanity.

The art of the icon was the creative response to this dilemma. It is possible to depict this mystery, but as no method of artistic representation which existed to date could do so, it was necessary to invent one appropriate to the challenge, which is what happened in Byzantium. Byzantium devised an art form in the icon, but also in its architecture, which stands even today as what Goethe called 'frozen music' of eternity, capable of incarnating two completely different natures in one hybrid form. It is almost as if the art form devised was a visible defeat of two of the three laws of logical thought: both the principle of identity and the principle of non-contradiction: everything is what it is and cannot, at the time it is what it is, be something else. And a thing 'A' cannot be both 'A' and not 'A' at the same time. Icons are both what they are and what they are not at the same time. This is not just a magical trick or an ancient form of *trompe l'oeil* art: it is a unique and *sui generis* art form which incorporates the paradox upon which Christianity is founded, namely the mystery of the Incarnation, whereby a fragment of the created world becomes the embodiment of a world beyond.

Of course the artists must use the same materials and methods that other artists use. In fact, icons owe a great deal to the contemporary artistic methods used for making effigies of emperors and other funereal monuments both in ancient Egypt and in Rome etc.[5] However, this does not mean that the iconographers of Byzantium did not succeed in doing something entirely new with these same materials and using these contemporary models. The icons of Byzantium forced artistic expression to perform a religious event which had never been as delicately encompassed in a work of art before that time. They fashioned out of wood and paint and lines and colours a way of encountering the face of Christ.

William Butler Yeats put his finger on the specific genius of the icons when he wrote that this art makes religious truths 'show as a lovely flexible presence like that of a perfect human

van Gogh: Sunflowers

van Gogh: The Yellow House

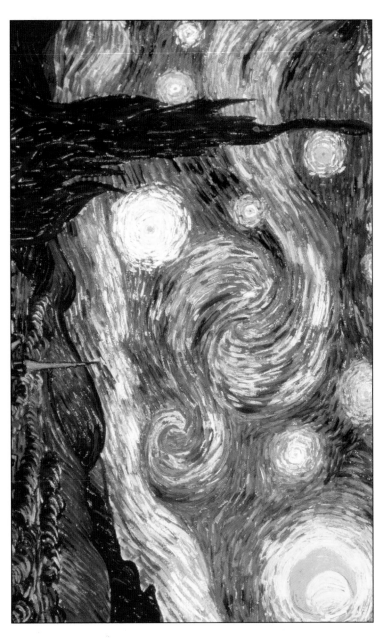

van Gogh: Starry Night

van Gogh: Self Portrait

van Gogh: A Pair of Shoes

Russian Icon of Virgin and Child with Saints

Sturge Moore's design for 'The Tower' by W.B. Yeats

Escutcheoned Door

body'.[6] The image of God is found in the human person: 'God created humankind in the image and likeness of Himself' as the book of Genesis puts it. And so, most icons are representations of human beings as revelations of the image of God; of human faces as the veils on which the imprint of divinity is most delicately sealed. And finally, of the eyes of human beings, as the most translucent and transparent windows to the soul, or that divine and infinite dimension of every human person: the eyes as doors of perception, windows to another world.

This has been described theologically by Florensky, one of the great Russian theologians:

> Whatever is occasional or conditioned by outer circumstances, whatever does not belong to the true 'face' is put aside by the energy of the image of God which, like a spring, has broken its way through the thickness of the material crust thus turning a face into the image. An image is a graphic reflection of the likeness of God on a human face.[7]

Art and religion worked hand in hand to overcome a problem never before encountered in the history of humanity: the mystery of God appearing in human form. Language had to be contorted and adapted over four centuries of intensive understanding to find words which could express this incommunicable event; art made parallel strides to undertake such representation in its own idiom.

Icon painters work according to strict rules and canons laid down for such painting and have to be people of prayer and contemplation who are able to discipline themselves into a frame of mind and a state of soul that allows them to be in direct contact, in their own lives, with that same spirit which they are trying to release in the work of revelation they are undertaking.

But what is it about the icons that is so special, so different? First of all their subject matter. This can be divided into three main categories, although others have extended this list to five and more. They are scenes from the Bible, both old and new testaments, which have a didactic purpose, as one might also see on the great stained glass windows of so many Gothic cathedrals. They are portraits, although not in the same sense that we have come to understand portrait painting since the sixteenth century and up to our own time. And they are 'apparitional'. This refers to those depicting all aspects of the mystery of the Incarnation, which surpasses anything that can be accounted for in the natural order and depicts the intertwining of the divine and the human as such as history unfolds in human terms. Icons depicting the Mother of God are of this kind, as are depictions of the Transfiguration, the Resurrection and the Baptism of the Lord. Such icons, because they break through the norms and boundaries of natural existence, are often perceived to be sources of divine intervention and are accorded even greater veneration than those in the first two categories.

In the icon, the figure of Christ, the Virgin Mary, the saint or whatever figure is being represented is the centre. The viewer is faced with a reversed perspective and it is the icon that is beholding you, not the other way round. This is why most figures are in a frontal position, with eyes gazing outwards like laser beams. Instead of being the source or starting-point of the picture as in perspectival painting, the beholder is the culminating or vanishing point of the icon.

There is little or no psychology or drama going on within the icon itself that the viewer can pry upon like a voyeur from the outside; most of the energy is being generated between the spectator and the figures in the icon itself. The place in whose forehead the gaze of the icon opens is you yourself.

In the icon we do not see God as an object to be contemplated but as a subject contemplating us as viewers. Thus, the icon does not try to represent God as he is in himself, but as he appears to us.

Technically speaking, there is no shadow, therefore, in the world of the icon. We do not find the subtle play of light and darkness we have become so familiar with and enchanted by in European painting. The layer of goldleaf which is the basis for most icons is the fundamental symbol of the presence of God as light. Gold is not really a colour, strictly speaking. It is a surface which eliminates all illusion of an intermediary space between it and the forms embedded in it: it is pure context. It absorbs into itself other light, even that emanating from other colours.

By all such methods icons are means of communication. They radiate an energy of light. They are not meant to create pious sentiments and/or psychological moods in the viewer; they are meant to be the most immediate (without media) communication: windows into another world.

The icon has no frame. It is not self-contained. It is open to the infinite on all sides. It is merely a focal point, a prism, a symbol, concentrating energy and relaying vision to a place beyond itself. The fact that it is a flat material surface is dissolved by the artistry accomplished on and through that surface.

William Butler Yeats
and Byzantium

The person who can best bring together the various threads being woven through this tapestry and who has influenced me most in my understanding of symbolism in art is William Butler Yeats. His presentation of this area of life, expressed most subtly and profoundly in his poetry, is difficult and punctilious. I shall use much of the detailed and profound scholarship of recent times to elucidate what I understand to be his original and essential contribution to a neglected area. In his work and in his life, Yeats brought us towards a clearer understanding of what images and symbols could mean and could achieve.

Ezra Pound had defined the image as 'that which presents an intellectual and emotional complex in an instant of time' and later expanded this attempt to brand the original species of wildness which he knew had been eliminated almost to the point of extinction by the twentieth-century manufacturers of thought, and which he believed passionately it was the task of the poet to revive and to rehabilitate. 'The Image is more than an idea. It is a vortex or cluster of fused ideas and is endowed with energy. If it does not fulfil these specifications, it is not what I mean by an Image.'[1] In this rehabilitation of what he calls the 'Image', using a capital 'I', Pound is distancing himself from the 'Symbolist' movement and more or less promoting the higher case 'Image' as a substitute for that overused and misleading term. Pound was trying to identify and recuperate the most potent idiom of artistic endeavour. More recent practitioners have added their own experience to such clarification.

One of the characteristic things about great works of art 'is that they can bear – and, indeed, that they invite – a superplenitude of possible readings, some of them contradictory'.[2] Symbols and imagery in art – as distinct from mathematics and science – eschew clear-cut definition, exclusivity and comprehensive precision, in favour of suggestive intimation and inclusive entrapment. The novelists Iris Murdoch and Roberton Davies describe such technique in their own works with enlightening and available imagery, using the image to trap the image itself. Murdoch's first novel is called *Under the Net* and she is asked whether this image means to explain her understanding of the image.[3] She replies that it is an 'obvious image for the understanding of particulars … One constantly desires to get "under the net" of language toward the thing itself.' Scientific symbolism targets the universal, the objective, what is a necessary fact for all people at all times. Artistic symbolism engages with the intimately particular, the specifically subjective. This requires of it to be ajar. Murdoch continues:

> It's open-textured, yes. The world comes in and out of it. You might think of it as a sort of pot with holes in it. Human life as we understand it, and the things that concern us at the moment, and how we see the world at the moment: these things all have to be seen in relation to the novel which endures. If you go on reading (say) *War and Peace* throughout your life, then it is like a different book at various times.

Robertson Davies picks up on such imagery: 'A truly great book should be read in youth, again in maturity and once more in old age, as a fine building should be seen by morning light, at noon and by moonlight.'

So, the imagery and symbolism of art are targeting a universality and objectivity quite other than science. Symbols here are not abstractions devoid of particularity and subjectivity, aiming at incontravertible validity; they are cryptographs which intimate the poignancy of the singular and the nerve-ends of sensitivity.

The later poems of Yeats were vehicles for the images which he received from the twenty-year process of religious endeavour, recorded more prosaically in *A Vision*. This implies more than that the contents of these poems are full of strange and bizarre pictures which make them piquant and esoteric. Yeats is attempting to formulate an inspiration received from elsewhere in a shape and structure of language which requires an originality, an ingenuity as idiosyncratic and pliable as that employed by the Byzantine artisans, required and permitted for the first time to hammer out the mystery of a God become Man.

Symbolic intimation in poetic form is Yeats's strategy of poetic expression. 'We would seek out those wavering, meditative, organic rhythms, which are the embodiment of the imagination' he proposes in the 'Symbolism of Poetry'. This idiom has been examined magisterially by Denis Donoghue:[4] 'His instrument is rhythm, presumably because human feeling, which seeks release in words and is outraged by the poor release it finds, sways to rhythm as to music.' Emotion, feeling, the heart, which are left out of most scientific calculation, find their scope more readily in a world of symbols. 'The difference between symbol and fact is that symbol is willing to be surrounded by an aura of personal feeling, different for each mind that contemplates it; the fact tries to insist that it be taken on its own severe terms.'[5]

Yeats learnt much from Arthur Symons who dedicated his book *The Symbolist Movement in Literature* (1899) to him. 'To name is to destroy, to suggest is to create' was Mallarmé's principle, according to Symons, and the most subtle instrument of suggestion was rhythm, 'which is the executive soul'. But Yeats was to take the symbol much further than his contemporaries of the so-called symbolist movement. Donoghue suggests that 'Yeats started out as a Symbolist and ended as something else'. This 'something else' is what this book is trying to identify in more concrete terms. Donoghue further explains:

> An image becomes a symbol, on being touched by value or significance not attributable to its own set. For example: think of an event in narrative as a moment or a position along a line, straight or crooked, and then think of it as being crossed by another line of value from another source. Each line is a set, a paradigm. But the event which occurs at the point of intersection between two sets is an image in both; its duplicity constitutes its symbolic force. Interpreted in one set, it declares itself unrestrained by that interpretation; it is part of the other set as well. When we find an image becoming a symbol, we feel in it this double potency; its allegiance expands, as if answerable to both idioms, ready to participate in both sets of relations. This marks its freedom and its suggestiveness; we have a sense in attending to it that there is no point at which we can say for sure that its force has come to an end.[6]

In 'The Symbolism of Poetry' Yeats says that 'all sounds, all colours, all forms, either because of their preordained energies or because of long association, evoke indefinable and yet precise emotions, or, as I prefer to think, call down among us certain disembodied powers, whose footsteps over our hearts we call emotions.' And in 'The Philosophy of Shelley's Poetry' he speaks of the Great Memory as 'a dwelling-house of symbols, of images that are living souls'.

Both Denis Donoghue[7] and Morton Irving Seiden[8] suggest that Yeats's poems were seen by him as a kind of liturgy. Yeats saw great art in general, and his own poems in particular, as embodiments of the supernatural. His symbols have theurgical power; his poems and plays are sacred rites. 'In a number of his essays, but notably in "Speaking to the Psaltery", first published in 1902, he urges that his poems be chanted or intonated as though they were (it seems) Orphic prayers.' By means of these supernatural poems 'he tried to recreate in the modern world the mythologies of ancient India, Eleusian Greece, and pre-Christian Ireland'.

In my own view, the ring-master in this circus of imagery has a task as complicated as shunting carriage-loads of animated and exploding jewelry along railway tracks from a signal box at a busy junction in an antique railway station. The signal box or cabin from which all such movement occurs is called, appropriately, 'The Tower'. Originally all such signalling was done by mechanical means: cables or rods, connected at one end to the signals and points and at the other to the signal box or other triggers, run alongside the railway. The guts of this system is a signalling frame, wherein one finds this complex cabling arrangement and linkage to levers and controls. A railroad switch is an installation provided at a point where rail track A divides into two tracks B and C. It can be set in either of two positions, determining whether a train coming from A will be led to B or to C. If we adapt this image to the 'system' which Yeats was trying to install, we find him also in a tower overlooking a junction where many more than three 'trains of thought' are merging. 'Central to the development of this elliptical and mysterious series,' says Foster about 'A Last Confession', 'is the subtle patterning whereby the interpenetrating gyres and cones of occult astrology are equated to the physical act of love: a fusion of the spiritual and the erotic which for Yeats connects not only to Swedenborgian cosmology but also to his early (and future) interest in Indian philosophy.'[9] But this is only one pair of opposites which symbolic representation is required to accommodate. There are others which are more varied.

The image as symbol is the vehicle, almost the stunt artist, which allows such ambidexterity to be conveyed without losing its integrity or betraying its illusivity. Can it be translated into logical thought? Helen Vendler thinks so. Her book, *Poets Thinking*,[10] defends poetry, because it is 'a feat of ordered language' as, therefore, 'something one can only call thought'.[11] Her 'criticism' of poetry has tried to elucidate the thinking of a poem as 'an exemplification of its own inner momentum' and in her chapter on 'W.B. Yeats Thinking' she claims to have cracked the code of his system of thought which she calls 'Thinking in Images' and which she uses as the subtitle of the same chapter. In justice, she claims 'we must call what [poets] do, in the process of conceiving and completing the finished poem, an intricate form of thinking, even if it means expanding our idea of what thinking is.' This 'thinking' cannot be revealed by 'a thematic paraphrase' for instance, but it can be excavated by the conscientious critic. Such a critic must be able to translate the subtle calculus of concatenated imagery into however distended an epistemology. What she describes as 'the complex architectonic assembling of images by Yeats' can be shown as his 'style of thinking' because even though it may become 'instinctual' in 'the heat of composition' it still 'issues from an extensive repertoire of image-memory and intellectual invention, coupled with an uncanny clairvoyance with respect to emotional experience'.[12] So, 'if we are to understand a poem, we must reconstruct the anterior thinking [always in process, always active] that generated its surface, its "visible core".'[13] Such 'thinking', described as 'the evolving discoveries of the poem', Vendler admits 'can be grasped only by our participating in the process they unfold'. However, in my view, she has already prejudiced such participation by limiting it to four comprehensive fields which she names as 'psychological, linguistic, historical, philosophical'. These exclude the very possibility, which the whole process was established by Yeats himself to explore – namely contact with a world outside all these fields which would come under the heading of 'religious, mystical, spiritual, magical'. Without at least countenancing such contact, there is little possibility of reconstructing 'the anterior thinking' of Yeats at whatever time or in whatever process he was engaged during most of his poetic life.

Yeats believed that true Christianity should be grafted to the indigenous religion of a country, that each country became a 'Holy Land' only when its imagination had been captured and its Old Testament led towards the expansive and comprehensive fulfilment of the new. Europe had no older or greater religious tradition than that embodied in the rites, the sites, the pilgrimages of pre-Christian, Celtic Ireland.

Byzantium, which symbolised for Yeats that perfect fusion of Christianity with the human imagination, in its early period, was contemporaneous with St Patrick (396–469). The 'unity of being' within a 'unity of culture' which Yeats regarded as the goal of religious reconciliation, was evident in the Book of Kells and other art works of this period of Celtic culture.[14]

In 1926 Yeats had written to Sturge Moore that 'what Whitehead calls the "three provincial centuries" are over. Wisdom and poetry return'. The two books of his poetry which probably best encompass these two life-giving realities are *The Tower* and *The Winding Stair*. And the two poems which set us, perhaps, upon the highest rock which Yeats was able to reach are 'Sailing to Byzantium' and 'Byzantium'. He wrote in *A Vision*: 'I think if I could be given a month of antiquity and leave to spend it where I chose, I would spend it in Byzantium, a little before Justinian opened St Sophia and closed the Academy of Plato.' The structure of *The Tower*, the book of poetry he published in 1928, is based upon the revelations which also informed that work he called *A Vision*. This book of poetry was named both for the poem of that title and Thoor Ballylee, the ancient tower house which still stands and which Yeats and his wife were converting into a symbolic home for themselves. This tower house in itself is important for a full appreciation of the symbol which the poet was hoping to leave behind him. Yeats also wanted this particular book of poetry, named after Thoor Ballylee, to be an icon in itself, and as itself. The real tower in which he lived, and the book of poems named after it, were part of the important legacy he would leave behind. He had asked Sturge Moore to create the design for the cover (see p. 111): 'The Tower should not be too unlike the real object or rather … it should suggest the real object. I like to think of that building as a permanent symbol of my work plainly visible to the passer-by.'[15] Three years later in a BBC Broadcast, which he made in Belfast on the 8 September 1931, he elaborated:

> Now I am trying to write about the state of my soul, for it is right for an old man to make his soul, and some of my thoughts upon that subject I have put into a poem called 'Sailing to Byzantium'. When Irishmen were illuminating the Book of Kells [in the eighth century] and making the jewelled croziers in the National Museum, Byzantium was the centre of European civilisation and the source of its spiritual philosophy, so I symbolise the search for the spiritual life by a journey to that city.

Sailing To Byzantium

That is no country for old men. The young
In one another's arms, birds in the trees
– Those dying generations – at their song,
The salmon-falls, the mackerel-crowded seas,
Fish, flesh, or fowl, commend all summer long
Whatever is begotten born, and dies.
Caught in that sensual music all neglect
Monuments of unageing intellect.

An aged man is but a paltry thing,
A tattered coat upon a stick, unless
Soul clap its hands and sing, and louder sing
For every tatter in its mortal dress,
Nor is there singing school but studying
Monuments of its own magnificence;
And therefore I have sailed the seas and come
To the holy city of Byzantium.

O sages standing in God's holy fire
As in the gold mosaic of a wall,
Come from the holy fire, perne in a gyre,
And be the singing-masters of my soul.
Consume my heart away; sick with desire
And fastened to a dying animal
It knows not what it is; and gather me
Into the artifice of eternity.

Once out of nature I shall never take
My bodily form from any natural thing,
But such a form as Grecian goldsmiths make
Of hammered gold and gold enamelling
To keep a drowsy Emperor awake;
Or set upon a golden bough to sing
To lords and ladies of Byzantium
Of what is past, or passing, or to come.
26 September 1926

Resurrection of the body is the artifice of eternity which Yeats was trying to describe. Such resurrection out of time and into eternity is a spiral movement which requires of us, and in us, both the protection and the artificial structure of the tower along with the inner spiral movement of the winding stair, 'for that supreme art which is to win us from life and gather us into eternity like doves into their dove-cots'.[16]

The Winding Stair should be seen as combining with *The Tower* in the same way that both the physical building and its internal stairway eat into one another and form the composite image of interpenetrating gyres. The world of eternity transforms the nature of our material world by drilling into it, as a sculptor drills into stone to form a marble eye. The second book contains the poem 'Byzantium'. Yeats was at one point going to make this the title of the book. Byzantium as an historical reality was the meeting place of two cultures that have formed the western world. The whole city, with its great dome and its mosaics which defy nature and assert transcendence, and its theologically rooted and synthetic culture, can serve the poet as an image of the Heavenly City and the state of the soul when it is 'out of nature'.

This was – especially at this time in his life and after a recent illness – really all that Yeats was now interested in. He writes in his diary in 1930:

> I am always, in all I do, driven to a moment which is the realisation of myself as unique and free, or to a moment which is the surrender to God of all that I am ... could those two impulses, one as much a part of truth as the other, be reconciled, or if one or the other could prevail, all life would cease ... Surely if either circuit, that which carries us into man or that which carries us into God, were reality, the generation had long since found its term.[17]

'Sailing to Byzantium' describes the first circuit, that which carries us into man. However 'Byzantium' attempts to describe the placement, the enactment and the reality of the second circuit, that which carries us into God.

Denis Donoghue shows how Yeats' play *The Resurrection* battles with a similar theme and quotes the sentence spoken by the Greek student of Heracleitus in that play, 'God and man die each other's life, live each other's death', as important commentary on the line in 'Byzantium' which speaks of 'death-in-life and life-in-death'.[18] It is as if 'Sailing to Byzantium' was about the first part of that double spiral and 'Byzantium' about the second. Yeats tells us that the second poem was partly inspired by Sturge Moore's letter on the inadequacy of 'Sailing to Byzantium.' Moore was

> skepical as to whether mere liberation from existence has any value or probability as a consummation. I prefer with Wittgenstein ... to think that nothing at all can be said about ultimates, or reality in an ultimate sense ... Your 'Sailing to Byzantium,' magnificent as the first three stanzas are, lets me down in the fourth, as such a goldsmith's bird is as much nature as a man's body, especially if it only sings like Homer or Shakespeare of what is past or passing or to come to Lords and Ladies.[19]

Yeats sent him a copy of 'Byzantium' so that he might design the symbolic cover for his new book, *The Winding Stair*, saying that Moore's criticism was the origin of the poem because his objection 'showed me that the idea needed exposition'.[20]

Byzantium

The unpurged images of day recede;
The Emperor's drunken soldiery are abed;
Night resonance recedes, night-walkers' song
After great cathedral gong;
A starlit or a moonlit dome distains
All that man is,
All mere complexities,
The fury and the mire of human veins.

Before me floats an image, man or shade,
Shade more than man, more image than a shade;
For Hades' bobbin bound in mummy-cloth
May unwind the winding path;
A mouth that has no moisture and no breath
Breathless mouths may summon;
I hail the superhuman;
I call it death-in-life and life-in-death.

Miracle, bird or golden handiwork,
More miracle than bird or handiwork,
Planted on the starlit golden bough,
Can like the cocks of Hades crow,
Or, by the moon embittered, scorn aloud
In glory of changeless metal
Common bird or petal
And all complexities of mire or blood.

At midnight on the Emperor's pavement flit
Flames that no faggot feeds, nor steel has lit,
Nor storm disturbs, flames begotten of flame,
Where blood-begotten spirits come
And all complexities of fury leave,
Dying into dance,
An agony of trance,
An agony of flame that cannot singe a sleeve.

Astraddle on the dolphin's mire and blood,
Spirit after spirit! The smithies break the flood,
The golden smithies of the Emperor!
Marbles of the dancing floor
Break bitter furies of complexity,
Those images that yet
Fresh images beget,
That dolphin-torn, that gong-tormented sea.
September 1930

In *The Tower*, Yeats made his home, Thoor Ballylee, an emblem of the imagination's constructive power. It is a symbol of the symbol. The book belongs to the first circuit. The second book, *The Winding Stair,* belongs to the second circuit and supplies the second gyre which is meant to move into the first and die with its life while it lives with its death. Imagination provides both circuits, but this is also because imagination itself is the one human faculty which is capable of circumscribing both. Both Yeats and William Blake believed that:

> this world of Imagination is the world of Eternity; it is the divine bosom into which we shall all go after the death of the Vegetated body. This World of Imagination is Infinite and Eternal, whereas the world of Generation, or Vegetation, is Finite and Temporal … The Human Imagination … appear'd to Me … throwing off the Temporal that the Eternal might be Establish'd … In Eternity one Thing never Changes into another Thing. Each Identity is Eternal.[21]

'Byzantium' is an experiment in articulating the poet's own reality, or shape, or image, after he is transfigured by death. Each of the selected images initiate him and ourselves into the mysteries which death delivers. In his 1930 diary, Yeats wrote a prose draft:

> Subject for a poem. 30 April. Describe Byzantium as it is in the system towards the end of the first Christian millennium. A walking mummy. Flames at the street corners where the soul is purified, birds of hammered gold singing in the golden trees, in the harbour [dolphins], offering their backs to the wailing dead that they may carry them to Paradise. These subjects have been in my head for some time, especially the last.[22]

'The soul has a plastic power, and can after death, or during life, should the vehicle leave the body for a while, mould it to any shape it will by an act of imagination, though the more unlike to the habitual that shape is, the greater the effort.'[23] In *A Vision,* Yeats wrote of Justinian's construction of Hagia Sophia (560 CE) as one of history's closest approximations to the ahistorical beauty of the full moon, phase fifteen of the gyre: 'Byzantium substituted for formal Roman magnificence, with its glorification of physical power, an architecture that suggests the Sacred City in the Apocalypse of St John.'

The characteristics of Byzantium are an almost complete dematerialisation, as if the city were manufactured out of air and shadowed on water, a deliberate destruction of the boundary between life and art – human beings are translated into mosaic, while symbols have the presence of 'a perfect human body; the beatitude of dead souls was realised there on earth.'

Resolution within the poem, as I read it, comes only in the last line, even in the last image: 'that gong-tormented sea.' The poet changes from the visual to the aural image.[24] Dematerialisation reaches its point zero on the dancing floor, without yet relinquishing its essentially human and passionate bodily texture, by delivering itself into rhythm, music, song. 'Song is existence', as Rilke has famously written. Yeats's poetry is the psalmody which will endure and which will persecute eternity. The gong has already appeared at midnight in the cathedral and the gong was also the aural image Yeats used for the effect which Maud Gonne exercised upon his earthly life. Whatever his love for her has meant, this is the keening sound which must linger into eternity if he is to survive his own mortality and perdure. Without the gong there is no remnant of passionate humanity. The gong is what secures everlasting remembrance of things past, in the otherwise bland and undifferentiated ocean of eternity.

Eternity becomes 'gong-tormented' by 'a slow low note and an iron bell'. This was the way Yeats described the reverberation throughout his own life caused by his meeting with Maud Gonne [gone/gong] 'a sound as of a Burmese gong, an overpowering tumult'.[25] It is as if he has agreed with Moore that any attempt to immortalise the songbird by fixing it in gold enamelling in mosaic or statuery is unworkable. Nothing of that kind can endure. Transverberation of eternity can only occur through sound. This last image of the poem harks back to the second verse of 'Sailing to Byzantium' where 'An aged man is but a paltry thing … unless soul clap its hands and sing, and louder sing/ for every tatter in its mortal dress'. The five verses of 'Byzantium' are coping with these 'tatters'. 'The unpurged images of day' have to wait for the second last line of the poem to beget fresh images which can release souls and the poem into eternity and infinity. The scenario of the poem takes place on the Emperor's pavement where 'complexities of mire and blood' achieve some purification and preparation for the journey to paradise. But even the 'agony of flame' is work of each one's imagination 'but her own conscience made visible'[26] not a real flame that might 'singe a sleeve'.

There is a mosaic on the pavement which represents dolphins and the great sea. This is Byzantine art which, like the poem, is a mixture of Greek, Roman and Asian elements, all of which combine to allow the viewer to pass into another dimension, the divine, the infinite, the eternal. All the verses up to the last line are concerned with the circuit which carries us into man. There is an ominous presence beyond, another greater ocean, which surrounds the pavement and which can flood. But the five verses deal with purification, with the attempt to purge the images of day. Such rummaging in 'the foul rag and bone shop' produces 'a heap of broken images'. They are smashed on the marble dance floor until at the last moment, as the ocean of infinity invades, they manage to beget fresh images which carry us into God. There are two fresh images, but these are enough to portray the new situation. It is as if this other reality in the background eventually overwhelms and the human soul, whose vehicle is the dolphin, tears open the ocean, before disgorging its reverberation into the deep. There is a sexual penetration of infinity implied in the image of the dolphin's dive. Each soul astride a dolphin's back returns to the deep with a reverberating resonance akin to that created in the soul of Yeats when he first met Maud Gonne. Eternity is torn and each penetration leaves its watermark. In drafts of the previous poem 'Sailing to Byzantium' there were dolphins in 'the foam/Where the dark drowsy fins a moment rise/Of fish, that carry souls to Paradise'. And it was originally a dolphin who would 'gather me/Into the artifice of eternity'.[27] Yeats was clear also that each soul was carried by its own particular dolphin. Moore's original design for the cover of the book in which Byzantium appears had all humanity riding on the back of one huge dolphin. Yeats wrote to him: 'One dolphin, one man.'[28] The shockwave caused by the dolphin's dive allows our bodies and our breath to make the impact of a gong. Dolphins use sound frequencies of natural sonar (an acronym, made up from the initial letters of _so_und _na_vigation and _r_anging) which emits ultrasound waves to localise things and communicate. Such acoustical oceanography is called 'echolocation'. A dolphin's signal frequencies can have an effect on the human brain by modifying brainwave activity. Their sonar language can travel hundreds of miles through the ocean.

Dying each other's death, living each other's life is here presented as a sinking into supernatural splendour, making a splash and a reverberation which infinity won't forget for a very long time – hopefully for eternity.

Part Three:

Liturgy

Liturgy

Religion is made up either of symbols or of activities that are mediated by symbols. Anthropologists and sociologists almost universally recognise the intimate relationship between religion and symbols. Clifford Geertz regards religion as part of a more universal cultural system. As cultural beings, we are symbolising creatures. He defines 'culture' as 'historically transmitted patterns of meanings embodied in symbols – a system of inherited conceptions expressed in symbolic forms'.[1] Religions constitute the institutionalisation of the general process by which a 'symbolic universe' is socially constructed and related to everyday social life. 'Sacred symbols relate an ontology and a cosmology to an aesthetics and a morality.'[2] This means that as human beings we are, more or less, programmed by our nature to devise for ourselves a satisfying explanation of the universe we were thrown into without our permission. This explanation cannot be the invention of one particular person, which is then imposed upon the community; rather it has to be convincing to the community as a whole. Only then can the world of art and of human behaviour derive from the symbolic life of this community. As a symbolic system, religion orders the universe, thereby eliminating chaos, ambiguity and helplessness.

Creating a World

At a dramatic level, the act of worship thereby creates a world. Obviously, no community is quite so naïve as to imagine that there is no world there until their liturgy takes place. That already-existing world is either an unformed world waiting to be invested with shape and meaning, or, more likely, it is a world that has already been created by some other liturgy, so that it has had some other meaning imposed upon it. There are many other modes of world-creation in which we participate and to which we are subject from our birth. These include advertising, ideology, propaganda, education and child-nurture. Most of these are ideologies imposed upon us by propaganda of one kind or another. 'World-making' for those who are seriously 'religious' can only be done by God. That is foundational to, for instance, Israel's faith. But it is done through human activity which God has authorised and in which God is known to be present. Walter Brueggemann has identified and nominated the particular stance, the precise posture, the prevailing attitude which marks off liturgical co-creation from the plethora of possible chicanery at either side of it. He calls it 'doxology', which means the right way to give praise to God, 'the strange power' of 'willing yielding' or 'the triumph of unconditional surrender'. Doxology, or the liturgy of 'praise', is our way of negotiating between the politics of ideology and the despotism of idolatry. It prevents us from being either 'idolatrous about heaven' or 'ideological about earth'. Praise is not a response to a world already fixed and settled, but it is a responsive and obedient participation in a world yet to be decreed and in process of being decreed through this liturgical act:

> Such praise is not abdication ... not resignation. Israel sings – untroubled and untempted by idols now defeated, unfettered and uncompromised by ideology now exposed. Israel sings committed to the subversion of the subversive God, prepared for a social possibility that outruns all our fearful necessities. Such praise is a yielding to the One who wants us never to submit to despair or in despair, but to yield to the inchoate but hinted possibility, never to submit to the present at the cost of the future.[1]

The liturgy enacts a different world. It sings the song of a world that is open, open to possibility. It uses symbols which are avatars of openness. Victor Turner defines a symbol as a 'storage unit', the basic 'molecule' of ritual activity. Ritual symbols are seen as 'multivocal' in that they may represent many things. Multivocality endows ceremonies, even those of the simplest form, with multiple levels of meaning. This in turn allows for the openness which divides the icon from the idol, the liturgy from ideology. The polyvalence of liturgical symbolism allows the multitude of worshippers to gather on the mountainside, and provides pliability for 'the inchoate but hinted possibility' to make its presence felt.

Christianity, however, is not a new religion, in some narrow sense of the word – it is a new form of existence. This existence is achieved by symbols and endures through symbols. It is the introduction of the dimension of resurrection into the spatio-temporal continuum. The breakthrough was accomplished on the first Easter day. Easter means resurrection. We are to rise from the dead. Not just on the last day, not just after our own bodily death, but now, *hodie*, today. 'You rose from the dead on the day you were born but you didn't realise it', Boris Pasternak has observed. 'Realising it' means making it real. Unless this happens for us we are not living the full Christian life. It happens for us through liturgy.

For the community gathered around Jesus Christ, Brueggemann again suggests it is the act of worship that is the act of world-formation. In its liturgical life the Church, led by the Spirit, engages in praise and obedience and so constitutes and is constituted as God's people. Liturgy is cooperative world-construction.

In the creation scene depicted in the Sistine Chapel in Rome, which Michelangelo completed in 1513, two years before Holbein moved to Basel, the life-giving finger of God, the *digitus Dei*, stretches out and almost – but not quite – touches the outstretched finger of the reclining Adam. Liturgy fills the gap between these two fingers.[2] It is a cloth of gold, a many-splendoured dream coat, woven like a cobweb between the fingertips of the human and the divine.

Resurrection is not some all-powerful divine act. It is rather the visible and tangible effect of the meeting and the union of divine love with human being. This connection is the miracle which God has always been trying to effect since the beginning of time and it is the reason why Jesus Christ entered our world. The difficulty is that we are hybrid creatures. Part of us is geared towards such connection but other parts of us are allergic to it. Resurrection means standing up and moving heavenwards. It can be symbolised by a vertical line, a tree, a totem pole, a steeple. Because this vertical line of resurrection is crossed by the horizontal line of heredity, biology, nature, the way we are by our human birth conflicts with the way we should be by resurrection. Such is the intersection we are trying to negotiate, the cross of human existence.

Biology fashions us in a way that militates against resurrection; it forms in us a particular will which crosses swords with the 'personal' will of our true spirit. Whatever the physical mechanism of heredity may be, it results in the imitation, voluntary or involuntary, of a ready-made model: instinctual conformity to DNA, instead of accomplishment of creative innovation. We prefer to live like ants or bees with an in-built code of behaviour, a blue-print for conducting our lives. Birth, marriage, death are the horizontal way. This is the natural pattern of human behaviour. So many dictators and perpetrators of ideologies have pandered to such natural tendencies and tried to force us into totalitarian juggernauts of another's design and construction. We are asked to take over the steering wheel and change that direction. We should be living creatively instead of conventionally. The way we do that is by switching over to the alternative energy of divine life. Liturgy makes it possible for us to do this on a daily basis. This does not mean that we repudiate what is natural and biological in favour of another, a better, a higher way of being. The principle of incarnation means that we achieve the incorporation into one unity of both dimensions. We move towards the infinite, the divine, the eternal, without damaging one tissue, without spilling one drop of what it means to be fully human, to be fully alive as men and women.

Exodus

But resurrected life does require some adjustment, some rearrangement of the way in which we live. It is the difference between living life as slaves in Egypt or as free agents of Exodus. The word *Exodus* in Greek means 'path out of' – escape route from the vicious circle of ourselves. Judeao-Christianity emerged from the Exodus. This became the identifying myth, the defining symbol of the march towards freedom, which, in terms of our human condition, has to mean progress towards what is unlimited and unconditional. Before this unimaginable event there was no people of Israel. The exodus from Egypt constituted the people of Israel. Before that event there was nothing but a scattering of disconnected people with no history, no reality, no identity. The exodus became the founding myth, the liturgical contour of the historical people. Even the account of the creation of the world in the book of Genesis, experts tell us, is a retrospective projection of the contours of the exodus experience onto the imagined emergence of the cosmos from chaos. The pivotal point in Israel's liturgical life is the continued reassertion of the astonishing claim that the gods are defeated, Yahweh rules, and therefore the world can act out its true character as God's creation. Israel constructs a very particular world that is different from and in direct tension with other available worlds. This very particular world is shaped according to the particular character of Yahweh, who convenes this world and who presides over it. The process of world-construction, in Israel as elsewhere, is a liturgical process. The work of the people in liturgy is to process shared experience through the normative narratives, images, metaphors and symbols of that community. Shared experience from one community is not unlike experience that is found in other communities. What is distinctive is the range of symbols through which the experience is processed. In its liturgy, Israel is engaged in processing its shared experience through its normative symbols and narratives. Valid world-making can be done only out of the materials that the community shares in its common experience.[1] Martin Buber describes the possible emergence of the original paschal liturgy, the way in which the exodus was celebrated liturgically, as follows:

> Favourable circumstances have, within a relatively brief period, provided a man possessing the character and destiny of a leader with the external prerequisites for the fulfilment of his immediate task, the leading of a group of semi-nomadic tribes out of the land of 'bondage'. The geographical and political conditions under which the impending wandering has to take place are tremendously difficult, no matter whether that wandering already aims at landed possession and settlement or, for the time being, at the resumption of a nomadic life. The human groups whom he proposes to lead out are only loosely associated with each other; their traditions have grown faint, their customs degenerate, their religious association insecure. The great thought of the man, his great impulse, is to establish a covenant of the tribes in the purer and freer atmosphere of the desert, which had once purified and freed him himself. And so Moses reintroduces the holy and ancient shepherds' meal, renewed in meaning and form.

The essential thing to realise, Buber suggests, is that here a natural and customary human activity – that of eating – is elevated by the participation of the whole community to the level of an act of communion; and as such is consecrated to God, is eaten 'for him'. However, such religious symbols cannot be merely arbitrary, or the specified protocol of some charismatic religious leader. They grow out of the individual or collective unconscious and, as Paul Tillich has suggested, 'cannot function without being accepted by the unconscious dimension of our being'. This is what makes liturgical symbolism antecedent to, and more potent than, any rational organisation or explanation.

> Out of what womb are symbols born? Out of the womb which is usually called today the 'group unconscious' or 'collective unconscious', or whatever you want to call it – out of a group which acknowledges, in this thing, this word, this flag, or whatever it may be, its own being. It is not invented intentionally; and even if somebody would try to invent a symbol, as sometimes happens, then it becomes a symbol only if the unconscious of a group says 'yes' to it. It means that something is opened up by it.[2]

Tillich holds that religious symbols do exactly the same thing as all symbols do, which is 'open up a level of reality which otherwise is not opened at all, which is hidden'. But this is not enough. If they are to reach the depths of reality which can be termed 'religious' they have to touch upon ultimacy. 'We can call this the depth dimension of reality itself, the dimension of reality which is the ground of every other dimension and every other depth, and which therefore is not one level beside the others but is the fundamental level, the level below all other levels, the level of being-itself, or the ultimate power of being.' Reaching this level actively in a way that allows for liturgical expression requires prophetic imagination. But such expression also requires the confirmation of the community, the *sensus fidelium*, or instinct of the faithful, whose discernment of revelation is guided also by the Holy Spirit.[3]

Martin Buber admits that we do not know what the original meaning of the term *pessah*, translated as 'passover', may have been:

> The interpretation of the 'leaping over' the houses of Israel by Yahweh, the 'destroyer' during the night of the death of the first-born is, in any case, secondary; even though at the time of Isaiah this supplementary meaning had become established. The verb originally meant to move on one foot, to hop. It may be assumed that at the old nomad feast a hopping dance had been presented, possibly by boys masked as he-goats. Just as there are war dances in which the desired event is portrayed and simultaneously trained for until the mime suddenly becomes a reality, so, it may be imagined, a symbolic representation of the Exodus may have passed into the Exodus itself.

This suggests that the 'symbol' was both the initiation and the repercussion of what eventually transformed itself into the exodus event. In other words, the intuition which Yahweh was trying to inspire in his people was delivered through a ceremonial rite, a dance, almost as a dream can provoke the daylight action to which it acts as prelude.

> Moses transformed the clan feast of the shepherds (the unleavened flat cakes are the bread of the nomads) into the feast of a nation, without its losing its character of a family feast. And now the families as such are the bearers of the sacramental celebration, which, however, unites them into a national community. Moses did not change

the custom of the ages into a cult; he did not add any specific sacrificial rite to it, and did not make it dependent on any sanctuary; but he consecrated it to Yahweh. He transformed the already existent Passover by introducing a new sense and symbol, as Jesus did later by the introduction of a new sense and symbol.[4]

It is this 'new sense and symbol' which is essential to understand.

Eucharist

The Church and the Eucharist, which establish the life of Christianity, are instituted by Christ and constituted by the Holy Spirit. Baptism, the Eucharist, the ecclesial community, establish our communion with the persons of the Trinity, energise our lives from eternity, burst through our space-time capsule and insert the oxygen of infinity, not just as an addition to, or a substitute for, our natural being, but as a transplant, a new creation, a relational metaphysics, a being as communion. What takes place is as miraculous, as revitalizing as a heart transplant. Each one of us becomes reenergised by the heart of God.

The self-emptying of our being as autonomous, self-possessed, lonely individual substance, to allow for this transplant and the consequent harnessing of our human source of love to the infinitely divine one, is necessary preparation. Egotistical me can be corroded by the quicklime of the Eucharist, allowing me to become what I already am by baptism, a member of this community of love. Our whole life is a 're-membering' of ourselves. This means that it takes us a whole lifetime to catch up with ourselves, to grow into the reality we have become by that mystery. We burst through our being in time to get beyond towards a new everlasting existence of love.

The Church guarantees that Christ is 'really present' not just in some ethereal or 'spiritual' way but in his flesh and blood reality every time the mystery of the Eucharist is celebrated. This involves an adequate and valid celebration with all the constituent elements in working order, whether or not I am present either physically or psychologically. This is what is meant by the much maligned formula *ex opere operato*. It means that God will not renege on this promise to be there no matter how deficient the presence may be at the other side of the equation, namely our side. Whatever else happens, God will be there.

So, we have to establish what exactly is necessary for an adequate and valid celebration of the Eucharist before we try to describe what actually happens once those conditions are met.

The problems multiply when we try to find out what exactly he did and what we now need to do in order to reenact it. Taking the complete panorama of evidence and reconstructing the original happening we seem to agree that the night before he died, Christ gathered his disciples around him and while they were having their evening meal he took bread, blessed it, broke it and gave it to his disciples saying: 'This is my Body.' Then in the same way, taking the cup of wine, he blessed it and gave it to them saying: 'This is my blood.' Then he further instructed them to 'Do this in memory of me'.

Later on of course, with hindsight and in retrospect, the disciples who were present and those who were not, began to read into this event all kinds of significance, most of which stemmed from the horrific outcome of that Thursday evening meal, when the celebrant was handed over to the authorities, tortured and crucified. It became clear that the actions he had performed the previous evening were ritual ones, whereby he was giving us his body and blood as a way of communicating with us beyond the reality of his impending death.

Later again, the followers of Christ realised that the meal during which Christ performed this extraordinary series of actions was in itself a Jewish liturgical celebration, a paschal meal, which itself was a ritual remembrance of the salvation of the Jewish people from the hands of their Egyptian masters, from slavery and subhuman existence. Where did this liturgical ritual spring from? Goethe's Faust aptly replies: '*Im Anfang war die Tat* [In the beginning was the deed].' 'Deeds' were never invented, they were done; thoughts, on the other hand, are a relatively late discovery. Ritual and liturgical expression come long before theoretical explanation or dogmatic theology.

In this way divine life is inserted into the circumference of human life. Biological life is horizontal and circular: time as birth, growth, decay, death. Resurrected life goes in the other direction. It introduces us to a different kind of space, *khora* instead of *topos*, as the Greek words describe, and to a different quality of time – *kairos* as distinct from *chronos*. Events rather than cycles are emphasised; milestones rather than metronomes; a freeze-frame tempo rather than a mere passage of time. We have to set our watches and our hearts to rise to such moments. Ready for ecstasy, poised for take-off. Putting in such a pacemaker is the work of liturgy.

Redeeming Time

Every year is cyclical, yet no one year should be the same as any other. Winter, Spring, Summer, Autumn. We derive our calendar from the Romans as we begin each year on 1 January, named after Janus, the God of gateways, whose festival was celebrated by the Romans at that time of year. July and August are named after Julius Caesar and his successor Caesar Augustus and we even accept that these months should have thirty-one days because Augustus, in a fit of jealousy, decided to lengthen his so that it would not be shorter than his rival's. To redress this balance, Augustus also decided that February should have only twenty-eight days. Februa was the festival of purification. Goats and dogs were sacrificed on the fifteenth day of the month (derived from the Anglo-Saxon word for the moon), when 'we' celebrated the fact that Romulus and Remus had been suckled by a she-wolf. Two naked youths, smeared with the blood of the sacrificed animals, raced through the city waving thongs of goatskin. If they hit any women with these thongs during their bloodstained caper, the gift of fertility would be conferred. Amazing that the names of these time-shares have survived. You would imagine that our more recent puritanical ancestors would have run a mile from such paganism. But, in truth, running a mile was also a Roman invention. A 'mile' was the Latin for a thousand and was taken to measure a thousand paces. Only at the end of the last century did we take to running metres.

September to December are the Latin names for seven to ten, *septem, octo, novem* and *decem.* Until about 150 BCE, the Roman year began in March. So, these last months were the seventh, eighth, ninth and tenth months after the beginning of the year each March. Mars was the god of war. April came from the Latin *aperire* meaning 'to open' because of the unfolding buds and blossoms of Spring. May was the goddess of fertility (Maia) and Juno, goddess of the moon. She also begins our week as Monday, the day of the moon. Depending on whether your language is English or one of the related Germanic languages such as German, Dutch, Danish or Swedish, the days of your week will be called after Teutonic or Norse gods and goddesses. French and other romance languages such as Italian and Spanish will derive their weekdays from classical mythology. Tiw of our Tuesday is a teutonic god identified with Mars (hence the French Mardi) as in *Mardi Gras.* Wodin or Odin and Thor, god of thunder, from the Nordic pantheon take care of Wednesday and Thursday. Frigg or Freya and Saturn are in charge of the weekend on Friday and Saturday. We are living in a carefully constructed world irrevocably encased in pagan time.

From earliest available records societies on this planet have based their measurement of time, their yearly calendars, on the movements of the sun and the moon. Most western countries now use the Gregorian calendar which was revised, from Julius Caesar's calendar, in 1582. This is based on the sun and the 365.242 days that the earth takes to circle it.

Hebrew and Muslim calendars are based on the moon. The first of these is dated from 3761 BCE, the year when the earth was supposed to have been created; the second from 622 CE, the year Muhammad moved from Mecca to Medina.

The truth is that we should not be prisoners under life sentence ticking off these dates, these years, in scratchmarks on the walls of our prison cells, putting down the time, wishing our lives away. Christianity has devised an alternative year, symbolising a different way of living time, which provides those of us who choose to be otherwise with a liturgical calendar, inserting the mysteries of Christ into the seasons and the times from Advent to Pentecost, allowing us to live these mysteries in a way that permits us to reap their benefit and switch over to the life of resurrection. Just as old-fashioned bicycles had tubes inserted between the wheel and the tyre which were then inflated to allow the person travelling to ride on air, so the liturgy provides a pneumatic (*pneuma* is the Greek word for 'air' and *pneu* the French word for 'tyre'!) insertion to the wheel of life which makes it possible to inhabit a capsule of eternity, and to live a life of resurrection, within the confines of whichever calendar year.

We have to sow a new harvest and keep on doing so day by day, year by year. Being naturally circular by tendency, we are children of the serpent, the serpent eating its own tail. In mesazoic times the planet was dominated by dinosaurs. We are their progeny. We take after them in so many ways. We are geared towards the secular year, the time measured by the gods of nature, who move us round in vicious circles.

To prevent the circle from being a perennially repeated error, we have to develop within us the movement upwards, the spiral. The spiral is the beginning of resurrection, the movement which transforms the flat and deadened circle into a curve. This spiral movement is generated and maintained by a life of liturgical celebration. Such a life is one that grafts itself onto the tree of life, which is the tree that is planted by the living waters of intercommunion between the Father, the Son and the Holy Spirit.

The tree as growth upwards and outwards is the model for such spiral growth. A tree could possibly grow along the ground, horizontally. And yet, it is drawn towards the sun, vertically. The compromise it settles for is a little of both. It grows both horizontally and vertically, a little bit every year. Every ring of the tree's growth represents one year of such movement, every tree ring contains a weather report for the year involved. Each ring describes a liturgical movement creating upward growth.

In a similar way, the time-space technology of liturgy inserts itself like an enzyme into the flat dough of ordinary time. It acts like yeast to raise that dough to a higher plane, while, at the same time, maintaining its integrity and preserving its identity as bread. The Church year could be said to begin in Advent. It awaits the coming of God, the insertion of the yeast, which is one of the images used for the arrival of the Kingdom of God. This event is eternal and, at the same time, it happens in time. Liturgy celebrates both and adds the further dimension of the third coming, which happens in me. Some liturgists doubt whether Advent is the beginning; others doubt whether the season of Advent should exist at all. It really makes little difference when the year of the Church begins. Liturgically speaking it begins today, every day, now, at this moment.

Advent

The word Advent designated originally not the period of preparation but the feast of Christmas itself. The coming of Christ in the flesh and the liturgical commemoration of that event was the *Adventus Domini*, the advent of the Lord. And since in the New Testament the word *Adventus* translated the Greek *Parousia*, it was natural that the term should include reference to the second coming of Christ at the end of time. Advent was a late development in Rome. The time of immediate preparation for Christmas, for instance, can be dated from 17 December. Before the Roman Advent was organised in the sixth century, the churches of Christian Gaul and Spain began their preparation for Christmas and Epiphany on this date. It was just three weeks before the Epiphany, a feast of very great importance for these churches, and a day on which baptism was conferred. So, for these churches, as for the Orthodox Christians, the important feast was Epiphany and not Christmas. Roman Advent was completed by the eighth century. Among the more splendid additions to this liturgy must be included the *O Antiphons* which have been in use in the western liturgy since the time of Charlemagne.[1] These seven preludes to Christmas sung before the Magnificat each evening at vespers epitomise, in the wide open vowel which characterises them and from which they are named, the expansive openness and availability of Advent symbolism. During this season, the liturgy uses imagery which allows many possibilities of emphasis and interpretation. The prophet Isaiah, who is a major spokesperson for the season of Advent, is quoted again and again as saying that 'the people who sat in darkness have seen a great light'. When he wrote these lines the people who were prisoners in darkness were the Israelites; their captors were Assyrian warriors. But these Israelites are more than that and the Assyrians are more than Assyrians. Assyria is a symbol for every power that is hostile to God and, at the same time, the quintessence of all inhuman oppression. Such imagery can travel through the ages of history and speak to every person who has been imprisoned in darkness. So, the German theologian, Jürgen Moltmann can be touched directly by these words of a prophet from 700 BCE 'when in 1945 we were driven in endless and desolate columns into the prisoner-of-war camps, the sticks of the guards at our sides, with hungry stomachs and empty hearts and curses on our lips'. And this symbolism invokes

> the millions of the imprisoned, the exiled, the deported, the tortured and the silenced everywhere in the world where people are pushed into such darkness.[2]

So, too, the symbolism of the exodus refers first and foremost to the people of Israel enslaved by the Egyptians and led out into the desert where they wandered for forty years until finally reaching the promised land. But, as a symbol, it refers to much more than that. It bespeaks the reality of every person who is enslaved by the spatio-temporal warp of natural life on this planet and who is eventually led to the possibility of eternal life as freedom from all limitation and captivity.

'The Church's *leitourgia*, a term much more comprehensive and adequate than "worship" or "cult", is the full "epiphany" – expression, manifestation, fulfillment of that in which the church believes, or what constitutes her faith.' I am using the words of Russian Orthodox liturgical theologian, Alexander Schmemann (1921–1983). Every liturgy is, in a certain way, a celebration of the Epiphany, the manifestation of God to God's people. Liturgy is where such manifestation happens. For St John, the Incarnation and the whole of Christ's life is presented as an epiphany. Christianity is a mystery of epiphany. The mystery takes place liturgically. All initiation, explanation, integration is 'mystagogical', which means that it can only be taught through these mysteries. So, Schmemann sees liturgy 'as the *locus theologicus* par excellence because it is its very function, its *leitourgia* in the original meaning of that word, to manifest and to fulfill the Church's faith and to manifest it not partially, not "discursively", but as living totality and Catholic experience'. The liturgy is not a book that we read, a ceremony that we perform, an illustration of some principle that we believe in; it is a deed that we do and one which makes immediately present the time and space of God's redeeming act, the three Persons of the Trinity involved in their rescue operation, here and now:

> And it is because liturgy is that living totality and that Catholic experience by the Church of her own faith that it is the very *source* of theology, the condition that makes it *possible*. For if theology is not a mere sequence of more or less individual interpretations of this or that 'doctrine' in the light and thought forms of this or that 'culture' and 'situation,' but the attempt to express Truth itself, to find words adequate to the mind and experience of the Church, then it must of necessity have its source where the faith, the mind and the experience of the Church have their living focus and expression, where faith in both essential meanings of that word, as Truth revealed and given, and as Truth accepted and 'lived', has its epiphany, and that is precisely the function of the *leitourgia*.[3]

If God came on earth to reveal to us the mystery of what it means to be fully human, this truth cannot be contained in formulae, catechisms, books or instructions. This mystery is transmitted liturgically. The divine love of the Trinity to which we are invited displays itself in our world through an idiom which is, at first, somewhat esoteric and alienating. In order to prevent itself from being cheapened, from being less than it was intended to be, it stands on ceremony. The liturgy invokes huge poetic licence when dealing with the mysteries which inspire it. For some liturgical traditions the emphasis of the Incarnation is the Epiphany, for others it is Christmas day. In the monastic antiphonary there is a kaleidoscopic mixture of imagery which proclaim at Vespers on the feast of the Epiphany that 'three great wonders fell on this day: today the star guided the Wise Men to the Child in the crib. Today water became wine at the wedding feast. Today Christ our salvation was baptised in the Jordan.'[4] This threefold 'today', as Peter Henrici points out,[5] is somewhat confusing since it encompasses a period of thirty years and does not even reflect the actual chronology of events. And the corresponding antiphon from Lauds of the same feast of the Epiphany only adds to the confusion: 'Today the Church was wedded to the heavenly bridegroom. In the Jordan, Christ washed her clean of her sins. The Wise Men hurry with gifts to the wedding of the king. Water is transformed into wine and gladdens the guests.'[6] Whatever about the chronology or the characters involved, what the liturgy celebrates here is the marriage of heaven and earth, 'the eschatological nuptial mystery', the love of God for us. The liturgy describes this in a fireworks display of imagery, a love poem, a wedding feast.

Liturgy and Life

The effect of divine love in us is to break the potbound periphery of our natural biological limitations and open us out through the cracks. We have to be broken open. The walls have to be razed. We have to be ploughed like earth being prepared for harvest. This applies to rules of logic and language as well as to biometrics and behaviour. Nor can these be achieved dramatically or instantaneously. They have to be approached delicately and in a long-term strategy of patient subversion. The passion of individualism which is instinctually in our nature as a necessity for self-preservation, self-promotion, self-fulfilment, has to be superseded by the movement which pours us out into the space between us and other people, accomplishing in us the capacity for real love, making us *Capax Dei*. Liturgy accomplishes such a delicate transformation as the wing of a butterfly might wear away a suit of armour by gentle and persistent caressing. It does this all day, every day, all the days of our life.

We are born individuals; we become persons by expansion of ourselves into the antechamber of the other. We have to have done for ourselves what God has already done for himself in our regard: break out of our natural mode of being and ensure that our nature no longer determines the limits of our personhood. Full realisation of our personhood is the specific work of the Holy Spirit, who inspires us to push through to that dimension of ourselves which is everlasting and unbounded.

It is not a question of either/or, of choosing this world or the next world, of selecting God or creation, of being human or being divine. It is a question of both/and. What is being proposed is not exclusion, denial, mortification, destruction of some particular element of what we are now, in order to develop some hybrid variation of ourselves, grafted onto the divine stem at a point above those areas which we intend to bypass or eliminate. The evolution which we must achieve will be a transformation and elevation of the whole human being to a level where the imperatives of biological reproduction will not be as pressing or as overpowering, but where the vocation to love will be more specifically human, more personal, more total. Such transformation must take time and space and must involve all the courteous precision of ritual, the conscientious persistence of ceremony.

It is a question of becoming fully human. Our reluctance is understandable. But the point is this: we were made to be persons in love; anything less is diminishment, deprivation, emasculation. The word 'person' was invented by Judaeo-Christianity to cope with the immense reality we were discovering about ourselves, because we had been chosen as love objects by God. As the caterpillar moves from chrysalis to butterfly, we too can move from biological life to resurrected life. The latter is accomplished through the power of love which changes us from individuals into persons. God came on earth to teach us the meaning of the word 'person' and the meaning of the word 'love'. Both lessons have to be taught and learned liturgically, although they are expressed in the world in which we live.

The world in which we live is to be understood neither as an organism nor as a mechanism but as a work of art. Resurrection is an art form. Much of that art is accomplished through liturgy. It is living, acting, doing miraculously, as opposed to 'naturally': it is walking on water, turning water into wine, liberating captives, restoring health, ushering in the Kingdom of God. Jesus Christ is love incarnate. He came on earth to institute the life of the sacraments which is the way of transforming our biological existence into resurrected life. This happens by sealing our verticality in several places in several different ways, to allow us to stand upright. We are talking about the kind of love that moves mountains, that works miracles, that pushes the human body to the limits of performance.

Science has now shown us that matter is energy at base. Your consciousness, your experience of being who you really are is energy. This energy does not just live in your brain; it fills your entire body. Your consciousness is connected to every cell in your body. Through your consciousness, you can communicate with every organ and every tissue.

Everything begins with your consciousness. Everything that happens in your life and everything that happens in your body begins with something happening in your consciousness. Sooner or later we will know that resurrection is a way of energising ourselves; it too is a question of consciousness. We have to move ourselves from the biological to the eschatological. Liturgy is the culvert which effects this transmutation.

We either continue to live naturally or we begin at each moment to live creatively. That is the meaning of miracle: stretching nature beyond itself. Evolution suggests, biology confirms, that we are the only species on earth which can bend itself towards whatever it chooses to become. We are architects of our future selves, of our own future. We can become whatever we choose to become. This does not just happen, it is done. It is an art work – truth that enters the world through human being.

We can enter from our own world into another world with an alternative time and space dimension. Almost in the way the children in C.S. Lewis's novel, *The Chronicles of Narnia: The Lion, The Witch and The Wardrobe*, find their way through an old cupboard in an old house into another world which is called Narnia (see p. 112). The film of this story uses the virtuosity of trick photography to present the viewer with a convincing version of such experience. The children enter the door of the wardrobe, feel their way in the dark, past clothes hangers, moth balls, fur coats, towards the back of the wardrobe. As they do so, the hangers change mysteriously into branches of trees and the floor and back wall of the cupboard are transformed into a vast snow-filled landscape. Such doors are available to us, although the transformation of liturgy is not as is displayed in this story. Our entry is not from one world into another world which would be a mirror image of the one we leave.

There is no Narnia as a replicated world above, below, or behind the world we live in. There is, however, a possibility of entering another time/space dimension, of living another kind of life if we are ready to embrace another kind of time, another kind of space – properties of this other kind of life which lasts forever. Liturgy is a process whereby we construct such a time/space pod. The Greek words *topos* as geographical place and *chronos* as calendar time help us to grasp the kind of time we are used to; their other two words *khora* and *kairos* suggest the further dimensions of time and place which are also available to us. We have only one word for these two realities which shows how one-dimensional we have become. *The Lion, The Witch and The Wardrobe* presents us with two worlds, both of which are topographical although the time suggested in both worlds is somewhat different. When the children enter the world of Narnia, the time in the real world seems to stop and they imagine that they are away for hours, even days, but find when they return through the cupboard that it is as if they had never left. The place which is Narnia is a mirror image of the world they have left. It has trees and snow, light and darkness, animals and people. There are differences, of course, but these are not sufficient to warrant a new kind of geography.

When we accomplish liturgy we do not enter another world as a replica of this one. The transformation which occurs, the making present of the Kingdom of God, is not a make-believe world hidden behind the spaces which we occupy; it takes place personally in the space inside each one of us. 'The Kingdom of God is within you.' We become transfigured from within as the dusty wardrobe is transposed into a sunlit forest.

> It implies an organic and essential interdependence in which one element, the faith, although source and cause of the other, the liturgy, essentially needs the other as its own self-understanding and self-fulfillment. It is, to be sure, faith that gives birth to, and 'shapes' liturgy, but it is liturgy, that by fulfilling and expressing faith 'bears testimony' to faith and becomes thus its true and adequate expression and norm: *lex orandi est lex credendi*.[1]

Over years of such transformation we eventually shed the cocoon which prevents us from spiralling heavenwards and forever. This is eternal life which happens liturgically as of now.

Liturgy as Mystery

Resurrected living is a form of love. Being and doing from this source is everlasting life. In ourselves, in our bodies, it shows as radiance. We are, and we act from, the true centre of ourselves. Such habitual living creates a feeling of standing on solid ground inside yourself, on a patch of inner eternity which even physical death cannot remove. Liturgy allows the life of the Trinity to circulate. It is breathing the Spirit. We embody this life in a way that transforms us into its icons. The Spirit is the artist who moulds us into our being as image and likeness of God.

The glory of God, as St Irenaeus has put it so succinctly, is any one of us fully alive, and 'orthodoxy', as the word tells us in Greek, is the right way to glorify God. This 'orthodox' way is liturgy. Essential to our task of resurrection is the establishment of real, lasting, indeed everlasting, contact with the living God. Through the economy of the mystery of the liturgy our nature becomes interpenetrated by the divine properties of being. The natural extinction of our bodily existence, when ingrafted to the body of Christ, is regenerated by an eternal energy which allows us to transcend the boundaries of our naturally limited personhood. The link between these two forms of personal life (ours and God's) is necessarily artificial like an iron lung or a prosthetic limb; it is an extended form of existence which establishes itself liturgically. Our expression of that new form of existence is a new song, is praise. We have no idea what life beyond the natural limitations of our being might be. We have to be tutored in this, as we have to be trained to walk the path of resurrected life.

True worship as praise allows us to open fully as flowers towards the sunlight, in the direction of the most High. Such an exercise is open to the past through inspired *anamnesis*, remembering the wonderful working of God in our own lives as well as in the evolutionary impetus of the planet; and open to the future through *epiclesis* (invocation of the Spirit) which diminishes our own agenda and disposes us towards God's originality. The platform from which we take our transport for such a journey is liturgy.

St Paul uses much of the terminology of a mystery religion when introducing us to the essence of Christianity. *Mysterion*, the mystery, is the eternal counsel (wisdom, *sophia*) hidden in God (Eph 3:9) – before ever the world came to be (1 Cor 2:7) – whose eventual manifestation will mean the end of this world (Eph 1:10). The apostolic mission is part of the unfolding of this mystery (Eph 3:2, 9) and Paul himself as steward of the mystery must be acquainted with these secrets, the gift of a prophet being to penetrate the mysteries of God (1 Cor 2:10; 4:1; 13:2) and become acquainted with all the mysteries. *Mysterion* (the hidden mystery) is connected with *Kerygma* (the proclaimed message) as the Father is manifested by the Son, who is an epistle (from the Greek *epi* + *stellein*, meaning 'to send') from God. So, all knowledge of God is a mystery both in the way it is communicated and the way it is received. No human agency has proprietory claims, production control, or distribution rights in this regard. The way a mystery is handed on is itself a mystery. Christ came on earth to reveal the mystery of that life which is lived eternally by the three persons of the Trinity. He replaced one mystery with another mystery. The only reality more mysterious than the three persons in one God is the reality of the human person. And this is the basis of our religion, the mystery on which it is founded. *Mirabile mysterium, magnum haereditatis mysterium*, the liturgical antiphons proclaim for us in song.

Tradition in the early Church was a fund of unwritten customs and mysteries making up the sacramental and religious life of the community (*ta agrapha tes ekklesesias mysteria*) necessary for understanding the truth of revelation and pointing to the mysterial character of Christian knowledge as a gnosis of God (*gnosis theou*) which is a gift conferred through such tradition.

Later, very much later, this oral tradition was written down and eventually hammered into dogmas and a credal formulae which became the *breviatum verbum* (the abridged version) as John Cassian[1] calls the Symbol of Antioch, making allusion to St Paul in Romans 9:27, who in turn is alluding to Isaiah 10:22. It was in the fourth century that the preferred rendering of the Greek term for mystery became 'sacrament' which referred most especially to Baptism and the Eucharist.

Christian liturgy has been called 'the cult of the Trinity': the way in which we accomplish in our space-time continuum the life of ever-expanding selflessness which is the invasion of our being by divine love. Christianity as ritual must be anchored in the time and space of the original event of resurrected life. That is why the 'mystery' is celebrated in a series of temporal 'mysteries' commemorating various moments in the life of the Second Person of the Trinity here on earth. This is what we mean by 'tradition' and this is also what we mean by humility. Humility comes from the Latin word *humus,* the earth. We are grounded in the real presence of the Risen Lord. Each 'mystery' is a real, experienceable occurrence in which something of God's hidden glory comes to light – for all those who have eyes to see and ears to hear – an escutcheon, in fact, the background meaning to the foreground event.[2]

'The liturgy, both in its totality and in each of its rites or actions, is symbol', Alexander Schmemann explains. But he makes an important distinction. Liturgy is 'the symbol, however, not of this or that particular event or person, but precisely of the whole mystery'. The mistake we have made is in applying to the liturgy a kind of symbolism which can be described as 'illustrative' which means treating the liturgy as a substance or a texture in which every element and every aspect has to be symbolic of some action or attachment attributable to the earthly life of Jesus Christ. Schmemann condemns liturgical symbolism of this detailed and applicable parallelism which verges on the fetishistic and which floods the essential symbolism with a plethora of rubrical red herrings. On the contrary, 'the entire liturgy is the symbol of the mystery of Christ's ascension and glorification, as well as the mystery of the Kingdom of God, the "world to come".'[3]

Liturgy is not just a finicky or fetishistic foible for sacristans or rubricists; nor is it a specialist field of research for paleography, history or archaeology. It is, as the Vatican Council II affirmed, the 'ontological' activity of the followers of Christ, 'the summit of the Church's activity, and the source of sanctification'. We have tended to reduce it to an abacus of pathetic correspondence which keeps us occupied at the level of crochet. Most of these correspondences are borrowed from a time when 'an abundant parasitic symbolism was flourishing'.[4]

Liturgy, as taught in seminaries, for instance, had so often degenerated into courses for future priests, teaching them how to perform the sacred rites of their ministry. By the time they had dealt with all the rubrics, which were endlessly detailed and precise, there was little energy or occasion to examine other aspects. Explanations of how and why the priest wore a specific attire became ludicrously embroidered with dubious and complicated symbolism. The Roman Pontifical, for instance, 'illustrated' the use of a mitre for bishops as symbolising the horns of Moses, comprising one horn for the Hebrew Testament and the other for the New Testament, both affording the said bishop with an appropriately awesome appearance. Even traditional clerical dress is derived from clothes worn by fashionable personages in ancient Rome. As fashions changed the tendency towards conservatism caused the Church to retain and beatify the original selection. Symbolic meanings have been applied which were not connected with the more practical decision to use such clothing in the first place. An example is the cassock which became the 'ordinary' dress of priests. It derived from a warm, long-armed garment worn by pre-Christian Celts known as a *caracalla*. Fashionable Romans despised it as vulgar barbarian dress until the Emperor Marcus Aurelius Antonius (211–17) decided to wear one to make himself more popular with his troops. Overnight it became high fashion. *Caracalla* became 'cassock' in English and it should 'ideally', when closed at the front, have thirty-three buttons for Roman Catholic clergy, symbolising each of the thirty-three years of Jesus' human life on earth, or thirty-nine buttons for Anglican clergy, symbolising the thirty-nine Articles of Religion.[5] The colour for both is black, which makes for another kind of symbolism, when worn, in the sweltering heat of sub-Saharan Africa, for instance, preferably with accompanying 'saturno' as headgear. We have traded the pearls for baubles and buttons.

Christianity is a living tradition. Its fundamental source is the Spirit who is ever-present and who breathes where the Spirit will, and who enjoys diplomatic exemption from any or all ecclesiastical forms or formulae. These remain close to the Spirit as long as they are not removed from such contact. Liturgy and the original oral accounts of what happened were always seen as *Prima Theologia*, whereas dogma and the credal formulae which synopsised these and turned them into propositions were understood as *Secunda Theologia*. Alfred North Whitehead puts it starkly: 'Religions commit suicide when they find their inspiration in dogma.' And Vladimir Lossky suggests that 'a doctrine is traitor to tradition when it seeks to take its place'. Dogmas are a safeguard, not a source. The word 'dogma' comes from the Greek for 'what seems right'. In essence, dogma proclaims that *Prima Theolgia*, the primary text, the liturgy, can mean this and this, but not that. They put a fence around the meaning to safeguard it from corruption or dilution.

Gadamer in his book *Truth and Method* reminds us that 'the general nature of tradition is such that only the part of the past that is not past offers the possibility of historical knowledge'.[6] The only way we can remember anything is through something which still exists in our contemporary world. There has to be some relic, remnant or historic remains which are with us today which allow us to determine the source of our historical knowledge, practice or belief. Nothing remains of the founding fact of Christianity except the effect it had on the survivors. How then does the tradition of Christianity survive? What is it that we remember? Symbols are the major source of our remembrance.

'Do this in memory of me.' Christ is remembered after two thousand years in a series of cultic actions which are known to the faithful as the Liturgy of the Eucharist or more popularly as the Mass.

An established liturgy emerged around the act of remembrance, and the various elements essential to a valid repetition of what the Lord had done were assembled and copperfastened into an established rite. Those of us who were Roman Catholics born before 1960 will remember the Mass to which we had become beneficiaries. This rite was a legacy from the Middle Ages and its content and form were hammered into a monolithic structure in times of persecution, heresy and religious warfare, which developed around them corresponding attitudes of triumphalism, dogmatism, fanaticism. It seemed as if the Tridentine Mass (receiving its name from the Council of Trent, which was summoned to elaborate the Catholic Counter-Reformation) was the God-given ritual whereby we were guaranteed to reenact the presence of Christ in his body and blood as he was really present at the Last Supper.

This ritual was and is very splendid, very consoling, very mystical. It had, and has, enormous attraction for generations of practising Catholics. And yet, it was full of dangers and deceptions, not least of which was the corollary that this was the only way of salvation and that it was all that was necessary for achievement of that goal.

What happens on the altar when we celebrate the Eucharist is a mystery. There are several approaches to mystery. We can treat it as a problem that has to be solved and can pursue it relentlessly until we have explained it adequately. Or we can abdicate all responsibility for making it accessible in any way, preferring that it remain totally incomprehensible and thereby even more mysterious. Mystery for the first category, like a mystery thriller, a detective story, keeps you guessing until eventually the secret is revealed, after which you lose interest and go on to the next chapter. You certainly don't go back over it again. The second approach is one of reverential awe and paralysed unworthiness. The mystery is mystery because I am dull, unclean and unworthy to understand it. Between these extremes there is a middle way. The mystery was intended for me, has no function, reality or significance without me. Therefore, unless I do everything in my power to prepare myself adequately and examine it thoroughly, it could pass me by without any impression or impingement.

There have been many attempts to 'explain' what happens during the Eucharist. Some of these make it sound like magic, others try to make it pass for science. Both approaches are understandable and natural.

The gospel words are startlingly simple: Unless you eat my flesh and drink my blood you shall not have life in you. And the night before he died Christ took bread, blessed it, broke it and gave it to his disciples saying: This is my body. And taking the wine he said: This is my blood. Do this in memory of me. Many then left him because this was too hard a saying.

How we explain this 'saying' and this reality is a choice of language, of images, of metaphors, of symbols. In both the scriptures and the early Christian attempts to explain what happened, the way in which God set out to give us his life, the mystery of our salvation accomplished by, with and through Jesus Christ, myriad images are used: pastoral imagery, Christ as the Good Shepherd; military imagery, Christ as conqueror; medical imagery, Christ as healer; sacerdotal imagery, Christ as high priest; sacrificial imagery, Christ as lamb of sacrifice; and legal or juridical imagery, Christ as redeemer (coming from the word as used today for buying back what we have mortgaged). All of these are attempts to explain a mystery; none of them have either a monopoly or even pride of place. The way in which we accomplish the mystery is necessarily symbolic. Liturgy is our way of 'doing' the mystery.

And yet, every element of the Eucharistic rite is 'artistic' in the sense that it occurs because someone decided that it should. These decisions may have been made in the light of some divine revelation or as some previously performed action of a divine person, but their actual presence and their performance or the way they either appear or are articulated derive from the work of human hands. From the moment we begin the ceremony, the way we begin, the way we process, the clothes, garments, robes we wear, the chants we sing, the candles, incense, insignia, accompanying officials; the building we use, the elements of the celebration, the altar, the disposition of the participants, the placing of the acoutrements, the linens, the cruets, the patens, chalices, books, the accompanying music, the rubrics of how and when we stand, sit, kneel, prostrate ourselves, enter or exit, and so on. Each one of these derives from some historical culture, depends upon some theological interpretation, results from some human decision about its appropriateness and its necessity for conducting the rite.

On the other hand, each one of these elements, actions, words, gestures, garments, implements, containers and paraphernalia should be examined constantly and replaced or removed wherever they are found to be mere quirks of human idiosyncracy or stubbornness. This applies more urgently to elements and additions which accrued from cultures and ages disrespectful towards certain members of the congregation who might have been discriminated against for their race, their sex, or their class. Any element of the Eucharistic ceremonial which fails to promote the dignity of the human person, the cultivation of the real presence of both the living God and every member of the participating congregation, which denotes any whisper of exclusivity, should be removed.

What Christ did was to give us his body and blood. This makes us partakers of his divinity, makes us lovers of his calibre, makes us alive in the way that he was alive, which means as resurrected bodies. He did this by taking elements of our created world, the ones that were to hand for an ordinary meal, the ones we constantly and regularly use to nourish the very bodies that he was trying to raise from the dead. These happened to be bread and wine because of the cultural circumstances in which the original meal took place.

'The glory of escutcheoned doors'

The quotation which gives its name to the title of this book comes from Yeats's poem 'Meditations in Time of Civil War'. He uses it in a context and in a sense quite other than mine. The word 'escutcheon' comes from the Latin word for a shield (*scutum*). An escutcheon can be the technical term for a shield with armorial bearings; or the middle of a ship's stern where the name is placed; or it can refer to the pivoted keyhole cover which has to be slid back either to insert a key or to peep through a keyhole. This last is my reason for choosing the title. In the world we enter at birth we are surrounded by layers and levels of such doors bearing on themselves the heraldic insignia, the watermarks, the imprint, the birthmark, brandmark, hallmark, of their maker. But also, if we have eyes to see and ears to hear with, offering a keyhole to another world beyond the immediately sensible one, if we can remember the password, the open-sesame to such wardrobes, wonderlands, treasure troves.

Nature, persons, artworks and rituals each in their turn and in their own way provide us with such openings. God the Father peeps through the portals of nature as creator; God the Son is present in every word that is uttered; God the Holy Spirit is the air-bubble in the hermetically sealed container which is each individual person. This inner cell can be penetrated once our essential mystery has been revealed to another person. Creation, Scripture, Tradition are the formal names we give to these three escutcheons of eternity, which are inserted into the doors of our workaday world.

Judaeo-Christianity is based on the presumption that God has spoken from outside our natural world. Such a 'message' is received by 'hearers' within our world. However, the 'revelation' is so extraordinary – outside the ordinary, natural, everyday spatio-temporal dimension of our world – that it enters our lives in something of the way a meteor might arrive from outer space and leave a gaping hole in the geography of our planet. The first witnesses of this eruption (for instance, Moses confronted by the burning bush) are so staggered and overawed by what they encounter that they have no epistemological equipment available which is adequate to the task of encompassing the experience in some comprehensive way. They act or react to what they have experienced long before they are capable of either expressing or explaining what has happened. Such actions or reactions, in turn, become the basis for ritual reenactment whereby the tribe or community of such 'hearers' try to harness for themselves the energy, the power, the benefits of such extraterrestrial visitations of which, through the particular 'prophets' or witnesses of the divine intervention, they have become unwitting beneficiaries.

Liturgy is a symbolic form of knowing which makes ritual activity into primal epistemology. Such knowing is quite opposite to the form of epistemology which we have learnt from modern science, which never begins from what we don't know to lead us towards what we might conjecture from such awesome experience. On the contrary, it begins always from what we do know, and do know with absolute certainty, upon which we are permitted to build a sure and certain system which explains our universe. Recently, the Archbishop of Canterbury, Rowan Williams, suggested that the liturgical way of knowing may be more paradigmatic in terms of describing the fundamental gesture and shape of our knowledge as human beings:

'The human system of knowing cannot be spoken of except as a spiral of self-extending symbolic activity … What is involved in knowing something is more like re-enacting a performance than labelling an object.'[1]

When we are born into this world we imagine that we have entered reality. The world we land in is the real McCoy. Are you a down-to-earth person with your feet on the ground? Are you for real? Are you living in the real world? Or are you a dreamer living in cloud cuckoo-land? We are taught to survive in the natural world. Science is the measure of all that surrounds us. We see, hear, taste, touch and smell the furniture of the stage set which we call our world.

But the possibility is that we have arrived into another womb. The womb of the world. That our development as human beings is threefold rather than twofold. That we go from larva to chrysalis to butterfly and that the natural world which we now inhabit, far from being the end of our journey is rather the crucible in which we are fashioned for eternity. The first womb was dark and we were passive. This second one is porous and we are hyperactive. The world we are about to enter is infinite and eternal. It can only suggest itself to us in our present intermediary condition by filtering hints into the cocoon of our incubator. If we are alive to such possibility we can pick up these hints and use them to prepare ourselves for the expansion and extension of our being which will be necessary to stretch us into the dimensions of eternity and infinity. The infinite and the eternal cannot fit themselves into a matchbox or an hourglass. They are by definition excluded from whatever is limited, enclosed, defined; whatever is temporal, momentary, time-serving. They surround the air-bubble of geographical space and local time without being able to invade it. If they did they would destroy its spatio-temporal identity causing it to flow out into unimpededness and extinction. We can only glimpse the reality which swirls outside our spaceship and which beckons us as amphibians (the word 'amphibious' comes from the Greek meaning capable of life, *bios* on both sides, *amphi* of the divide) to flex our muscles and exercise our latent but dormant limbs which will allow us to fly heavenwards or swim oceanwards, depending on whatever limited imagery we care to use, which will always be borrowed from our own spatio-temporal epistemology. There is nothing inside the time-space capsule which can even provide an inkling of what exists outside. And yet the outside itself can bruise or stain or pierce the paraphernalia of the inside sufficiently to leave a trail of clues to those with enough sensitivity, those with stereoscopic vision, to detect its presence. Such bruising, staining, piercing, echoing is what we call revelation. The skin that is bruised, the wool that is stained, the ears that are pierced, the canyons or caves that are echoed into are what we call symbols. The word comes from the Greek *ballein,* meaning 'to throw' and *sym* or *syn* meaning 'with', 'together', 'at the same time'. A symphony brings sounds together; a synagogue simply brings (*agein*) together (*syn*); syntax arranges (*tassein*) together; synods provide a way (*hodos*) together; sympathy is feeling (*pathos*) together; symbols are whatever is thrown against eternity and forever afterwards bears the mark of that bruising encounter, Jacob's thigh or Veronica's veil. Symbols are the things of this world which are drenched with some dew of endless night; impregnated with energy of eternal revolution; scarred with birthmarks of fingerless midwives; stamped with the imprint of verisimilitude; steeped in the aura of divine intervention. Incarnation of God in any or every leaf of the universe. Those who have eyes to see and ears to hear, noses to smell, fingers to touch, tongues to taste, get the message. It is stereoscopic vision: seeing the trees for the wood.

Such understanding is not simply sensuous, subjective, physiological, nor is it abstract, objective, metric. It belongs to the order of mythical consciousness which is somewhere in between these two extremes. The 'mythical' world view effects a construction of space and time which is analogous to, although never identical with, the construction of geometrical space and the building up of objective 'nature' in science. It too operates a schema through whose mediation the most diverse elements, elements which at first sight seem incommensurate, can be brought into relation with one another. Between two realms there occurs a kind of exchange, a perpetual transition from one to the other. 'The totality of the scientific cosmos is a totality of laws, i.e. of relations and functions.' The merely sensuous world which we taste, touch, see, hear and feel around us is 'poured into a spatial mould' through which it is 'apprehended in accordance with the universal laws of geometry ... In contrast to the functional space of pure mathematics the space of myth proves to be structural'.[2]

In liturgy as in mythological thinking 'regardless of how far we divide, we find in each part the form, the structure of the whole ... The whole spatial world, and with it the cosmos, appears to be built according to a definite model, which may manifest itself to us on an enlarged or a reduced scale but which, large or small, remains the same. All the relations of mythical space rest ultimately on this original identity; they go back not to a similarity of efficacy, not to a dynamic law, but to an original identity of essence.'[3] The time-space world of liturgy is structural in this sense but also in the more recent understanding which 'structuralism' as a movement in contemporary philosophy has offered. In 1916 Ferdinand de Saussure claimed that there was a general science of signs, which he called semiology, which would take any system of signs, whatever their substance or limits; images, gestures, musical signs, objects, and the complex associations of all these which form the content of ritual, for instance, which would constitute a kind of language which would be, at the very least, a system of signification. It should be possible to uncover the 'deep structures' of any such system. More than that: any 'reality' or 'truth' is a construct of the language employed to describe it. Claude Lévi-Strauss demonstrated the potential of this Saussurian model of language to understand all our cultural expressions. From these two we may adopt the maxim that liturgy is a form, not a substance, and should be analysed in terms of its internal structures rather than from its content.[4] These insights, it seems to me, were present in Alexander Schmemann's attempt to distinguish between illustrative and eschatological symbolism.

> 'Makes present.' It is precisely this function that the later illustrative symbolism begins to lose, and precisely to the degree that it becomes merely illustrative. The reason for this is that people apply to the liturgy their particular vision rather than seeking in the liturgy the vision implied in its own structure and texts, in short, in its own symbolism. The term which best expresses the initial liturgical experience of the Church, the experience which shaped and also maintained and preserved the fundamental order of worship, is 'eschatological symbolism'. The word 'eschatological' refers to the belief, central and overwhelming in the early Christian community, that the coming of Christ, his life, his death and Resurrection from the dead, his ascension to heaven and the sending by him, on the day of Pentecost, of the Holy Spirit, have brought about the Lord's Day, has inaugurated the new *aeon* of the Kingdom of God. Those who believe in Christ, while they still live in what the New Testament calls 'this world', already belong to the new; for, united to Christ and anointed with the Holy Spirit, they have in them the new and eternal life and the power to overcome sin and death.[5]

Liturgical symbolism is 'eschatological'. If I could explain, and if you could understand, these four words, we would have accomplished the purpose of this book. So, do not run away before the end. We have to use words when we are explaining to each other, and sometimes these words are clumsy and ungainly because our vocabulary has been unable, as yet, to find expressions which are more compact and transparent. Eschatology in Greek means the logic of what is meant to happen to us all in the end. The liturgy realises, makes real, the whole mystery of completeness, the meaning of everything that is, the perfection of what was intended from the beginning of time, by, for, with and through the creation of the world.

This reality is the work of the Holy Trinity, Father, Son and Holy Spirit, who have been working towards this consummation since the Spirit first brooded on the immensity of waters and the platform of the world was put in place. The second Person of this Trinity became a human being and in his bodily life on earth, realised the full potential and everlasting viability of what it means to be a human being. He left behind him on earth the guaranteed foolproof identikit (the 'do this in memory of me') for each one of us to become fully alive ourselves. Not by becoming like him, not by imitating what he did, not by assuming his temperament, his characteristics, his particularity. On the contrary, the essential and the complementary work of the Holy Spirit is to allow each one of us, in different times, in different places, and in different ways, to apply and to integrate what Christ *is* – his being rather than his having or doing or behaving – into the specific reality of who we are. We give birth to Christ in our lives, at the deepest point in ourselves. That is why the Virgin Mary is the parallel, precursory yet contemporary, female manifestation of the same human reality accomplished by, through and with the Holy Spirit. She actually gave birth to Jesus Christ in the way that each one of us is required to do symbolically. Male and female, we *are* in the image of God, symbols of the ultimate potential which each one of us can reach. Our person is potentially infinite, eternal, divine, if we allow ourselves to be blown into those dimensions by the power, by the breath of the Holy Spirit. Because the 'person' as such is infinite, eternal, unique. And the essential gift of Christ to the Father and to the Holy Spirit was, is and always will be the gift of ultimate personhood. He emptied himself of everything else, his race, his country, his singularity, his history. He reduced himself to what was unique, essential, universal, to the point zero of human identity. From this ultimate point, his humanity could be fully assumed into his person as eternal, infinite, divine and shared with us, who share his human nature. This is the ultimate meaning of the Assumption of the Virgin Mary. She has become fully what we are also invited to become.

The liturgy is the enactment of this mystery of personhood, the ritual representation of an eternal gift accomplished in the historical lifetime of one particular Jewish man in the course of his ordinary, lowly, undistinguished and short human life, which ended in his peremptory and violent execution. Liturgy is neither a morbid nor a celebratory dwelling upon the past. It is a making present (a 'representation' in the fullest sense of the word) of the eternal and infinite reality accomplished by, with and through that unremarkable life, a reality which is from *now* onwards available to all of us, if we allow ourselves to become part of the divine energy which enabled all this to happen in the first place.

We become what we celebrate; that is the logic of the eschaton.

> The whole point of eschatological symbolism is that in it the sign and that which it signifies are one and the same thing. The liturgy happens to *us*. The liturgical entrance is our, or rather, the Church's entrance to heaven. The entire liturgy is the Church's ascension to Christ's table in his kingdom, just as the Eucharistic gifts sanctified by the Holy Spirit are the Body and Blood of Christ. And we do

all this and we are all this because we are *in Christ*, because
the Church herself is our entrance, our passage into the
new aeon bestowed upon us by Christ's incarnation,
death, resurrection and ascension.

We celebrate what we become, now, at this moment, and forever
afterwards. It is not something out there which we touch and
taste and smell and see like works in an art gallery or
performances in a concert hall. It is something we step into like a
new element, which we allow to encircle and to penetrate until
we become saturated like seaweed. From the outside in, it is
something which we eat and drink, we absorb and assimilate,
until it enters our bloodstream and eventually takes over as the
alternative energy running our lives. Liturgy holds and provides
an imagery, a geometry, a symbolism which can be shared by
those who have gone before us. It allows the possibility of
communion, commensalism with the dead. It goes further and
suggests that there is a whole area of consciousness, not just
between birth and death, but between death and rebirth, which
can be logged into.

The symbols are things we put on, assume, sink down into,
absorb. We do not face them and approach them as parts of a
greater reality which is behind or beyond them. We experience
them as elements into which we disappear, over which we hover
until we evaporate, against which we nestle until basted. 'Every
moment of your life is the moment of Baptism', St Basil reminds
us. Every time and place in which we celebrate the liturgy is
further steeping in eternity, basking in infinity. Our death
should simply be the final wearing away, dissolution, distension,
absorption. The symbols of the liturgy are granules of a matrix
into which we shall eventually be osmosed without thereby
losing our defining personhood.

Liturgical symbolism effects in us the reality which it
represents. We become what it proposes. Transubstantiation is

not simply descriptive of what happens to the bread and wine which become, through liturgical celebration, the body and blood of Christ; it also describes us who also become the body and blood of Christ. Our taking and eating, our drinking of the blood of Christ transforms us from the natural individuals that we are into the resurrected persons that we become. Divine love as resurrectional energy is incorporated into our bodily organic system, into our bloodstream, and this energy eventually transforms us into what we have consumed. We become what we eat and drink. This also transforms our connections with each other. We become points on the outer circle which describe the resurrected body of Christ, the work of the Holy Spirit. We become one body not by our horizontal relationships with each other as we may, or may not, hold hands together around the altar, but rather as radii of that same circle which meet and join at the centre, the *culmen et fons* of every liturgical celebration which is Christ, through the Holy Spirit, returning to the Father.

End Notes

Annapurnas of the Mind

1. Gerard Manley Hopkins, 'No worst, there is none', the Oxford Authors edition edited by Catherine Phillips, OUP, 1990, p. 167.

Knockfierna

1. Matthew Stout, *The Irish Ringfort*, Dublin, Four Courts Press, 1997.
2. This 'melancholy biographical poem' was written for his old school magazine. *W.B. Yeats, The Poems*, edited by Daniel Albright, London, Dent, Everyman's Library, 1992; rev. edn 1994, p. 349.
3. Kathleen Raine: *W.B. Yeats and the Learning of the Imagination*, Golgonooza Press, 1999, pp. 5–6.
4. W.B. Yeats, 'An Acre of Grass', *Collected Poems*, London, Macmillan, 1955, p. 347.
5. R.F. Foster, *W.B. Yeats: A Life*, I: *The Apprentice Mage 1865–1914*, Oxford University Press, 1997; II: *The Arch-Poet*, 2003.
6. John Carey, 'Poetic License,' *The Sunday Times*, 9 March 1997, sec. 8, p. 1.
7. A.N. Whitehead, *Science and the Modern World*, New York, Mentor, 1960, p. 57.
8. Walter J. Ong is the first of these. His book is called *Orality and Literacy, The Technologizing of the Word*, London & New York, Routledge, 1982; this edition, 2000. Hereafter in this text referred to as (Ong + page number).
9. Ernst Cassirer, *The Philosophy of Symbolic Forms*, Yale University Press, 1955. Volume I: *Language*; Volume 2: *Mythical Thought*; Volume 3: *The Phenomenology of Knowledge*; Volume 4: *The Metaphysics of Symbolic Forms*.

10. Ibid, Volume 2, pp. 83–85.
11. Ibid, p. 424.
12. Ibid, p. 431.

Harry Potter and the Three Rs

1. John Killinger, *God, The Devil and Harry Potter*, New York, Thomas Dunne, 2003.

Art

1. Much of what I say here about the symbolist movement is taken from Michael Gibson, *Symbolism*, Cologne, Taschen, 2006.

The Day the Earth Moved

1. Derek Wilson, *Hans Holbein: Portrait of an Unknown Man*, London, Pimlico, 2006, p. 1.
2. Dostoyevsky, *The Idiot,* Penguin Edition, p. 447.
3. For a meditation on the novels of Dostoyevsky in this regard cf. my article 'The God of Tolstoy, Dostoyevsky and Solzhenitsyn' in *The Crane Bag*, vol 7, no 1, 1983, pp. 65–73.
4. At the time of writing an exhibition has been mounted in the Tate Britain in London called *Holbein in England*. It concentrated on the artist's two periods working in London. He emerges here as one of the greatest Renaissance painters who ever worked in Britain.
5. Writing of the Holbein exhibition at the Tate Britain in *The Guardian*, Tuesday, 26 September 2006.

Holbein's Secret

1. Susan Foister, Ashok Roy and Martin Wyld, *Making and Meaning: Holbein's Ambassadors*, London, National Gallery Publications, 1997.
2. G.H. Villiers, *Hans Holbein: The Ambassadors*, London, Gallery Books, no 18, undated.
3. London & New York, Hambledon and London, 2002.

Vincent van Gogh

1. 'Religions pass away, but God remains.'
2. Quoted in Kathleen Powers Erickson, *At Eternity's Gate: The Spiritual Vision of Vincent van Gogh*, Cambridge, UK, 1998, p. 46.

3. Ibid, p. 59.
4. Ibid, L133, July 1880, *Letters* I: 193. Quoted on p. 66, Kathleen Power Erickson. In all other cases I have given the date of his letters referring to *The Complete Letters of Vincent van Gogh*. 3 vols. Introduction by V.W. van Gogh. Greenwich, Conn., New York Graphic Society, 1958. These letters can be found, with a few exceptions, more recently and accessibly in *The Letters of Vincent van Gogh*, Penguin Classics, 1997.
5. 'You have to represent what is everlasting in what is transient.'
6. Cf. Meyer Schapiro, *van Gogh*, New York, Harry N. Abrams, 2003, which is a concise paperback edition of *Vincent van Gogh*, published in 1969.
7. Martin Gayford, *The Yellow House, Van Gogh, Gaugin and Nine Turbulent Weeks in Arles*, London, Fig Tree, 2006.

A Pair of Worn Shoes

1. Jacques Derrida, *The Truth in Painting*, University of Chicago Press, 1989, p. 329.
2. Ibid, p. 260.
3. This last pious thought comes from Ken Wilber who uses this account of Gaugin's description of the shoes to develop his own 'holonic' theory of art interpretation and from whom I take the details of Gaugin's intervention. Cf. Ken Wilber, *The Eye of Spirit*, Boston, Shambala, 2001, pp. 110–114.
4. Ibid, p. 115.
5. This last interpretation was suggested to me by Stacy Wirth at the ISAP Jungian Odyssey Conference in July, 2006.

The Icon

1. Exodus 20:1-17: 'You shall not make yourself a carved image or any likeness of anything in heaven or on earth beneath or in the waters under the earth; you shall not bow down to them or serve them. For I, the Lord your God, am a jealous God.'
2. I am supported in these views of iconoclasm by Christophe Schoenborn in *L'Icône du Christ, Fondements Théologiques*, Paris, 1986, from whom I borrow some of these thoughts.
3. Cf. Colossians 1:15: 'He is the image of the invisible God' (where the Greek word used is 'icon') and Hebrews 1:3: 'He reflects the glory of God and bears the very stamp of his nature.'

4. Denzinger 653, p. 218, Can. 3. *'Sacram imaginem Domini nostri Jesu Christi et omnium Liberatoris et Salvatoris, aequo honore cum libro sanctorum Evangeliorum adorari decernimus.'*

5. Cf. Andre Grabar, *Christian Iconography: A Study of its Origins*, which were the A.W. Mellon Lectures in the Fine Arts at the National Gallery of Art in Washington in 1961, Bollingen Series, Princeton University Press, 1968.

6. W.B.Yeats, *A Vision* (1937) p. 279.

7. P. Florensky quoted in: *Icons, Windows on Eternity*, op.cit., p. 155.

William Butler Yeats and Byzantium

1. Quoted in *Imagist Poetry*, ed. Peter Jones, London, Penguin Books, 1972, p. 40.

2. Lawrence Weschler, *Vermeer in Bosnia: Cultural Comedies and Political Tragedies*, New York, Pantheon, 2004.

3. From *A Tiny Corner in the House of Fiction: Conversations with Iris Murdoch*, ed. Gillian Dooley, University of South Carolina Press, 2003.

4. *We Irish: Essays on Irish Literature and Society*, University of California Press, 1986, pp. 35–51

5. Ibid.

6. Ibid.

7. 'The basic assumption is that souls do not die and therefore may be evoked. Correspondingly, the *anima mundi* is not merely a store of images and symbols, it is what a race dreams and remembers. The great soul may be evoked by symbols, but spirits are not mere functions of ourselves, they have their own native personalities. So the best reading of the *anima mundi* is that it is the subjective correlative of history, a nation's life in symbols; it is not our invention, but may respond to our call, if, like the mage, we speak the right words. He must go on perfecting earthly power and perception until they are so subtilized that divine power and divine perception descend to meet them, and the song of earth and the song of heaven mingle together.' Ibid.

8. Morton Irving Seiden, *The Poet as a Mythmaker 1865–1939*, Michigan State University Press, 1962, pp. 286–7.

9. R.F. Foster, *W. B. Yeats: A Life*, Oxford University Press, Volume II: *The Arch-Poet*, 2003, p. 319.

10. Helen Vendler, *Poets Thinking*, Harvard University Press, 2004.

11. Ibid, p. 3.

12. Ibid, p. 118.
13. Ibid, p. 119.
14. Cf. Kathleen Raine, *Yeats the Initiate*, London, George Allen and Unwin, 1986.
15. Ibid, p. 314.
16. W.B. Yeats, *Mythologies*, London, MacMillan, 1959, p. 301.
17. Donoghue quotes this passage to show that 'In prose-moments Yeats was prepared to concede, of Self or Soul, that one is as much a part of truth as the other, but in most of the poems he enlisted under one banner and for the time being served it zealously. In *The Winding Stair*, when it came to a choice between the circuit which carried him into man and that which carried him into God, he chose man; but even as he voted he felt the burden of misgiving, loss, sacrifice, waste. The longing expressed in the Diary points directly to "Byzantium" and *The Resurrection*'. Ibid, p. 77.
18. Denis Donoghue, *We Irish*, p. 78.
19. *W.B. Yeats and T. Sturge Moore: Their Correspondence 1901–37*, ed. Ursula Bridge, New York, Oxford University Press, 1953, p. 162.
20. Ibid, p. 164.
21. Quoted in Frank Kermode, *The Romantic Image*, London, Routledge, 1957, p. 89.
22. W.B. Yeats, *Explorations*, London, Macmillan, 1962, p. 290.
23. W.B. Yeats, *Mythologies*, London, MacMillan, 1959, p. 349.
24. This suggestion is somewhat less isolated and presumptuous in the light of recent research by Nóirín Ní Riain in her doctorate thesis *Theosony: The Sound of God*, University of Limerick, 2003.
25. *W.B. Yeats: The Poems*, ed. Daniel Albright, London, Dent, Everyman's Library, 1992; rev. edn 1994, notes no. 4 p. 718.
26. Ibid, notes 27, pp. 719–720.
27. *W.B. Yeats, The Poems*, ed. Daniel Albright, London, Dent, Everyman's Library, 1992; rev. edn 1994, notes no. 4, p. 720.
28. *W.B. Yeats and T. Sturge Moore: Their Correspondence 1901–37*, ed. Ursula Bridge, New York, Oxford University Press, 1953, p. 165.

Liturgy

1. Clifford Geertz, 'Religion as a Cultural System' in *Anthropological Approaches to the Study of Religion*, ed. M. Banton, London, Tavistock, 1966, p. 6.
2. Clifford Geertz, 'Ethos, world view, and the analysis of sacred

symbols' in *The Interpretation of Symbols*, New York, Basic Books, 1973, p. 127.

Creating a World

1. Walter Brueggemann, *Israel's Praise*, Philadelphia, Fortress Press, 1988, pp. 26–28, 153–156.
2. I borrow this comparison from Robert Taft, 'What does Liturgy Do? Toward a Soteriology of Liturgical Celebration: Some Theses', *Worship*, 66, no 3 (May 1992) p. 194.

Exodus

1. Walter Brueggemann, *Israel's Praise*, Philadelphia, Fortress Press, 1988, pp. 26–28.
2. Paul Tillich, *Theology of Culture*, New York, Oxford University Press, 1959, pp. 58–59.
3. This notion was included in two decrees of the Second Vatican Council: *Lumen gentium*, The Dogmatic Constitution on the Church, 12 and *Dei Verbum*, Dogmatic Constitution on Divine Revelation, 8. It derives, in Christianity, from John 16:13 and 1 John 2, 20, 27.
4. Martin Buber, *Moses: The Revelation and the Covenant*, New York, Harper Torchbooks, 1958, pp. 69–72.

Advent

1. Vincent Ryan, *Advent to Epiphany*, Dublin, Veritas, 1982.
2. Jürgen Moltmann, *The Power of the Powerless*, SCM Press Ltd, 1983.
3. *Liturgy and Tradition, Theological Reflections of Alexander Schmemann*, ed. Thomas Fisch, New York, St Vladimir's Seminary Press, 1990, pp. 39–40.
4. *Tribus miraculis ornatum diem sanctum colimus: hodie stella Magos duxit ad praesepium: hodie vinum ex aqua factum est ad nuptias: hodie in Jordane a Joanne Christus baptizari voluit, ut salvaret nos, alleluia.*
5. Peter Henrici, 'The Miracle of Cana' in *Communio*, Spring 2006, pp. 5–10.
6. *Hodie caelesti sponso juncta est Ecclesia, quoniam in Jordane lavit Christus ejus crimina: currunt cum muneribus Magi ad regales nuptias, et ex aqua facto vino laetantur convivae, alleluia.*

Liturgy and Life

1. *Liturgy and Tradition, Theological Reflections of Alexander Schmemann*, ed. Thomas Fisch, New York, St Vladimir's Seminary Press, 1990, pp. 39–40.

Liturgy as Mystery

1. John Cassian, *De Incarnatione* VI, 3. Cf. also St Augustine, *De Symbolo* 1; St Cyril of Jerusalem, *Catechesis* V, 12.
2. Cf. Peter Henrici, 'The Miracle of Cana' in *Communio*, Spring 2006, pp. 5–10.
3. *Liturgy and Tradition: Theological Reflections of Alexander Schmemann*, ed. Thomas Fisch, New York, St Vladimir's Seminary Press, 1990, pp. 39–40.
4. Dom Bernard Botte, 'The Role of Liturgical Theology', *St Vladimir's Seminary Quarterly*, 12, 1968, pp. 170–173. 'The Roman liturgy became "fixed" in the XIIIth century, i.e. at a time when "an abundant parasitic symbolism was flourishing".'
5. Richard Taylor, *How to Read a Church*, London, Random House, 2003, p. 228.
6. Hans Georg Gadamer, *Truth and Method,* New York, Continuum, 1989, p. 289.

'The glory of escutcheoned doors'

1. Rowan Williams, *Grace and Necessity*, London, Continuum, 2005, pp. 137–138.
2. Ernst Cassirer, *The Philosophy of Symbolic Forms*, Yale University Press, 1955. Volume 2: *Mythical Thought,* p. 88.
3. Ibid, p. 89.
4. I have found the clearest introduction to this difficult area of contemporary philosophy in two books by Richard Kearney, *Dialogues with Contemporary Continental Thinkers* (1984) and *Modern Movements in European Philosophy* (1986), Manchester University Press.
5. *Liturgy and Tradition, Theological Reflections of Alexander Schmemann*, ed. Thomas Fisch, New York, St Vladimir's Seminary Press, 1990, pp. 123–128.